Walking Blind

Walking Blind

Essays on Faith

Revised and Expanded Edition

Robert L. Canfield

WIPF & STOCK · Eugene, Oregon

WALKING BLIND
Essays on Faith
Revised and Expanded Edition

Copyright © 2025 Robert L. Canfield. All rights reserved. Except for brief quotations in critical publications or reviews, no part of this book may be reproduced in any manner without prior written permission from the publisher. Write: Permissions, Wipf and Stock Publishers, 199 W. 8th Ave., Suite 3, Eugene, OR 97401.

Wipf & Stock
An Imprint of Wipf and Stock Publishers
199 W. 8th Ave., Suite 3
Eugene, OR 97401

www.wipfandstock.com

PAPERBACK ISBN: 979-8-3852-4252-8
HARDCOVER ISBN: 979-8-3852-4253-5
EBOOK ISBN: 979-8-3852-4254-2

VERSION NUMBER 11/25/25

All Scripture quotations, unless otherwise indicated, are taken from the Holy Bible, New International Version®, NIV®. Copyright © 2011 by Biblica, Inc.™ Used by permission of Zondervan. All rights reserved worldwide. www.zondervan.com.

To our memories of Rita,

advocate, critic, sometimes opponent, faithful friend, celebrating sixty-two years of adventure together.

Contents

List of Figures | viii
Acknowledgments | ix
Invitation | xi

1. Walking Blind: A Promise to the Dismayed | 1
2. The Walk of Faith | 18
3. Why I Believe in the Resurrection | 31
4. Legal Certainty, Ethical Cowardice | 40
5. Biblical Advice on Nonreligious Living | 49
6. Social Revolution in the Two Letters to Philemon | 58
7. Political Uses of Religious Zeal | 72
8. Peter's Little-Noted Statement About Peoples "From Every Nation" | 76
9. "My God! You Are a Mussulman Man Like Me!" | 85
10. The Authority of Twelve Jewish Men | 99
11. The Greatest Social Critics of All Time | 107
12. The Bang and the Glory | 113
13. A Strange Prophetic Sign of the World in Crisis | 118
14. Biblical Sources of the First Amendment | 124

Bibliography | 131
Index | 135

List of Figures

Figure 1: Individuals with Paul | 66
Figure 2: Individuals in the Target Community | 67
Figure 3: Individuals Arriving with the Letters | 67
Figure 4: Global Land-Ocean Temperature Index | 120

Acknowledgments

THE INFLUENCES IN MY life have been many and diverse. I wish so many of my dear friends were alive to know how much I appreciate them, miss them and owe them. Their influence is evident in the places where I expose my soul. Of course, those folks were too numerous to be named, and virtually all of them are gone. I wish I could tell each one face to face how much I admired them and learned from them. I cherish my memories of them.

For this project I am fortunate to have had several accomplished friends. Reese Watt, founder and owner of Action Flow Software, graciously read and commented on drafts of several of these chapters. Our lunches together sharpened my perspective on what I was doing. And his encouragement kept me wanting to finish the project. My brother, James Canfield, applied his sixty years of experience in the computer industry to produce and promote this book. He chose the cover of the first edition and is already actively setting up a website from which the book is being launched. Robert Lowes, retired journalist and accomplished poet, has helped me escape the jargonistic style of academia. From him I am learning better how to attract and keep the attention of my reader. I hope what I have learned from him will be manifest to him throughout these pages. My daughter, Kim Canfield Kackley, undertook the role of my publicist. I never knew what a publicist was until I got the benefit of her many creative ideas. Ted Chafin of the WashU library was helpful in gaining access to necessary

Acknowledgments

sources. The comments on the first edition of this work by a group organized by W. Robert Binns, WashU Research Professor Emeritus of Physics, encouraged me to believe the book was worth revising and bringing up to date. Of course, the person whose influence was large in every part of this project was my wife, Rita. Her love, support, and forgiveness gave everything I did a sense of joy for sixty-two years. To all these people, I express my sincere gratitude. Together, their support helped me believe this project was not a waste of time.

Invitation

FOR MANY YEARS, I have had the habit of reading through the Bible, using its various writings as a source of my search for anchorage, authenticity, and self-acceptance. Many texts have helped me find encouragement, wisdom, and stability despite a restless, unquiet, fearful inner self. The proclamations, examples, enjoinders, claims and promises of the Bible have influenced my thoughts and sensibilities, and so shaped the way I have approached the deep questions of existence that on a subliminal level vex all of us. Having read through it several times, I find that certain passages of the Bible now evoke memories of situations past, when I was trying to work through feelings of defeat, embarrassment, doubt, fear, despair, or disorientation, when a particular example, teaching, or event in a passage stimulated thought, suggested possibilities, or introduced perspectives by which to work through my immediate crises. Some passages directed my attention to matters of higher substance and away from myself; some exposed self-serving preoccupations I should avoid; some effectively described or illustrated feelings of anxiety or shame I could identify with; and some reminded me of the broader moral context of my life, directing me to step back from the immediate preoccupations of the moment and to refocus my gaze toward the general context and enduring significance of my existence. And besides these common influences on my experiential world the Bible has, at times, presented issues so vividly that they induced me, again, to rethink or reconsider the way I have thought about myself and my dilemmas, and my opinions about affairs in our times. And I keep making discoveries. Occasionally, when I have reread a familiar passage, a sentence or paragraph would stand out to me, iridescent, with a message, a perspective, or an implication I had missed in previous readings.

In any case, my objective in producing this book has been to show that biblical writings can be relevant to anyone trying to live productively and justly in the conflicted and often ambiguous challenges of the contemporary world. The issues that drove folks in ancient times to write about their experiences, and their sense that the Creator had somehow been involved in their affairs, were not unlike the issues that plague every one of us—doubt, fear, defeat, disappointment, embarrassment, confusion, the collapse of the certainties we had lived by—and so their writings can awaken in us as contemporary readers creative ideas for how we might deal with our respective predicaments.

The Bible includes works of many genres, written over a span of several hundred years by individuals from various stations of life, a collection so diverse that no characterization of it as a single work is possible. Owing to its ancient origins, its diverse styles, and (in many cases) the circumstantial purposes of its authors, it can seem opaque and forbidding to the beginning reader. What I offer here are my reflections on a few passages of the Bible, some of them, relatively little discussed, in the hope that they will encourage others to look thoughtfully into this treasure trove of ideas that we call the Bible.

These essays were composed at various times as opportunity afforded—mainly on quiet Sunday afternoons (but once while I was trapped in the middle seat on a long flight).

Chapter 3 on the resurrection was written many years ago for *HIS Magazine*. The title essay was delivered to a group of professional adults in Pakistan. Chapter 9 is an extended version of the article of the same name that appeared in *On Knowing Humanity*, volume 9, issue 1, January 2025 (CC BY 4.0).

INVITATION

    These writings arise from many years of a private moral quest for a sense of significance in the world. I hope these chapters will inspire you to explore the Bible yourself as a fecund body of writings through which to nourish your own search for a sense of place in the world.

1

Walking Blind
A Promise to the Dismayed

As modern technology improves, horizons of increasing numbers of people expand. Their social and economic contacts are enlarging. Time and activity are compressed. The escalating pace of improvements in communications and transportation widen the range of opportunities. More than in any previous generation, people are developing more contacts, improving their skills and education, traveling more often, and to ever more distant and exotic places.

This broadening of opportunities can be exhilarating, but it often has the opposite effect. An increased variety of choices heightens the difficulties of choosing the one best choice. There are so many options, so many possibilities for the use of our time, skills and resources, that we can be dismayed. Every decision seems to foreclose all other options. The choice of one career seems to deny other interesting ones; the choice of a life mate excludes all other attractive individuals; the purchase of a house, a car, or whatever excludes other purchases.

Resources are always scarce relative to the possibilities. In fact, the expansion of possibilities exposes how resource poor we are. The opportunities afforded by modern society, with all its wares, have not simplified the important decisions we have to make; they often make them more difficult.

Moreover, after we have made a crucial decision, we may feel hemmed in by the conditions that result. As new dilemmas and challenges emerge from choices already made we can be boxed into situations that become odious. Even if in the abstract the range of choices is large, for most of us the truly feasible options can be excruciatingly narrow. We feel locked into circumstances beyond our control.

Some of us live with conditions we hardly know how to bear. And even those of us who enjoy reasonable prosperity can be obliged by an unforeseen event to change plans, lose opportunities, perhaps even watch situations ruined, relationships ruptured, and visions shattered. A feature of the modern world seems to be a fragility of meaningful relationships, an impermanence of social contexts, and an uncertain sense of place in the world.

Either way, whether we happen to confront a range of choices that are bewilderingly diverse, or whether we happen to be locked into circumstances beyond our control, with dreams and hopes for the future shattered by unimagined or unforeseen turns of events—in any case, despite many modern conveniences and much seeming promise, we can feel both cast adrift and imprisoned. We can lack a sense of anchorage or secure place, without a certain and incontrovertible reference point by which to orient ourselves in a shifting world.

My wife Rita and I have often had such feelings. We have sometimes felt overwhelmed by a complicated range of choices on a vital issue, and at the same time felt constrained by circumstances that seemed agonizingly narrow. Sometimes we have been unsure where we belonged, where we should go, what we should do, as a swirl of uncontrollable situations bulldozed our dreams and visions. And as Christians, we pondered whether our choices were according to God's will. "What does God want in this situation?" "What is God doing?" "Why is God allowing this?" Obviously, God is not confused; he doesn't change his mind; he is not surprised by the issues we confront; he is not limited to circumstances that seem to hem us in. And he has not abandoned us, despite our feelings, when our visions evaporate like the dew.

The Christian wants to learn how to find anchorage in God despite the continual shifting of relations in the contemporary world. A particular verse, has in this regard, helped us in times of confusion and doubt, even in despair, by providing a sense of anchorage when circumstances were painful and opportunities limited, and when wise decisions seemed crucial.

> I will lead the blind by ways they have not known, along unfamiliar paths I will guide them; I will turn the darkness into light before them and make the rough places smooth. These are the things I will do; I will not forsake them.[1]

The first time this promise struck me with particular force was when I was drafted into the army. The draft notice was a huge interruption in my plans. The notice forced me into a situation I expected to loathe and would have done anything to avoid. It meant two years of my life would be wasted (but probably without danger; this was before Vietnam). It was at this time that God's promise in Isaiah to lead the blind along unforeseen paths, making rough places smooth, seemed to speak directly to my situation. Through this promise God seemed to be saying that he was in control of my life and affairs; he would be with me through this "darkness" (as I saw it); and he would do new things in my life, despite the digression (as I saw it).

The clause "I will lead you in paths you have not known" suggested that there could be a purpose in this seeming waste of time. As it turned out, those two years were among the most significant in my life, for apart from other gains from the experience I met and married a wonderful woman. Since then, in the years that Rita and I have been together, when faced with disappointing developments, when forced to detour from activities and plans we thought important, when forced to deal with problems that seemed to come out of nowhere, to interrupt our plans, we have found comfort in

---

1. Isa 42:16.

this promise. It has often reminded me that God does not forsake us but is a source of strength, stability, and direction when we face "crooked" turns in our affairs.

THE CONTEXT

"I will lead the blind by ways they have not known," God says to the Israelites. He will be with them "in paths they have not known." It was a promise to a people caught up in a world they had failed to foresee, even though, in fact, they had been repeatedly forewarned. This verse appears in a section of Isaiah that can be read as specifically addressed to the Israelites in their exile—that is, after Jerusalem was destroyed, after the survivors had been forced to leave the only world they knew and become servants of their conquerors in Babylon. They were at this time living as exiles far from home.

There are specific references to their exilic situation in this part of Isaiah. Their temple, built by Solomon, has been burned to the ground.[2] They have suffered grief and humiliation. But now Cyrus and the Persians had defeated the Babylonians and in 539 BC, invited the Jews within his domains to go back to their homeland. He had even encouraged them to rebuild their temple in Jerusalem and sent back some of the precious objects taken from the first temple. And the prophet is encouraging the exiles to make this hazardous move.

The actual time when this section of Isaiah (chapter 40 to the end) was written is disputed, as Isaiah himself, friend of Hezekiah, lived well before the exilic period. Many scholars date this section to a later author, perhaps to a tradition of authors who consciously cherished and propagated the writings of Isaiah. Somehow their writings were added to Isaiah's original text. Other scholars regard this part of the book of Isaiah as a production of the great prophet himself. They believe its strikingly graphic images of the exilic period were written prophetically under the inspiration of the Holy Spirit long before they would take place. This dispute is of no major concern to my treatment of this text here, as both groups

2. Isa 64:10–11.

agree that the text had a special significance for the Israelites in their exile.

I want to examine it as a text with specific relevance to the Israelites in that period, in their exilic contexts. In this sense, the exilic experience was (as every Israelite experience in Scripture) a kind of parable of the human condition. The Israelites in their suffering are an archetype of every one of us in a state of alienation and exile.

It is not uncommon, and it may be increasingly so, for people to sense that the world has lost order and is spinning out of control. This promise to lead the blind in new, unfamiliar paths, to make darkness light and rough places smooth seems especially poignant for our times because it is so directly aimed to people whose world has caved in and whose life no longer makes sense.

HOW THE HEBREW KINGDOMS CAME TO RUIN

In the period before the collapse of Jerusalem, the two Hebrew kingdoms, Israel and Judah, had fallen into decline. In the northern kingdom of Israel, Jeroboam had introduced golden calves to be worshipped as the gods who delivered Israel out of Egypt.[3] Israel had a series of kings who were uniformly unfaithful to Yahweh, and only a few of the kings of Judah sought to honor Yahweh. Because of the indifferent commitment of the Israelites to Yahweh, prophets began to proclaim Yahweh's word to the Israelites, but they received little heed from the people, especially from the elite.

The prophets would eventually be honored, and their writings cherished, but in their lifetimes most of them were treated with indifference, if not hostility. And even after the kingdom of Israel fell to the Assyrians in 722 BC—an event that should have caused alarm in the kingdom of Judah—the rulers of Judah made little attempt to return their people to the sole worship of Yahweh. Manasseh (687–643 BC) polluted the sanctuary of Yahweh by bringing into the temple the symbols of worship to Tophet and

---

3. 1 Kgs 12:25–33.

other Canaanite gods. The temple built by Solomon and dedicated to Yahweh with great solemnity became a shelter for cult prostitutes, male and female, who served alien gods.[4]

By this time, the people of Judah and Israel had drifted so far from God that they had effectively forgotten the Mosaic tradition. The Torah, the books of Moses, which gave specific directions for the Israelites, had fallen into such disuse that the elite of Judah didn't recognize it when it was found in the temple during the time of Josiah (640–609 BC). When the contents of the book were read to Josiah, he was disturbed because many of the cult rituals forbidden in the Torah, specifically in Deuteronomy, were commonly practiced among the people of Judah. Josiah's attempts to reform were serious but short-lived, and soon after his untimely death, it was evident that many Jews were again worshipping the foreign gods that had been forbidden under his rule.

Indeed, there was much confusion about which gods to worship. People were unsure which god and which rituals worked best at saving them from the hardships of everyday life. After the destruction and burning of Jerusalem, some Hebrew women told Jeremiah that such a catastrophe had occurred because they had left off worshipping a Canaanite god whom they called "the Queen of Heaven." They told Jeremiah, "We will certainly do everything we said we would: we will burn incense to the Queen of Heaven and will pour out drink offerings to her just as we and our ancestors, our kings and our officials did in the towns of Judah and in the streets of Jerusalem. At that time we had plenty of food and were well off and suffered no harm. But ever since we stopped burning incense to the Queen of Heaven and pouring out drink offerings to her, we have had nothing and have been perishing by sword and famine."[5]

It was to Israel and Judah in this period of decadence that many of the great Hebrew prophets were sent. Through Isaiah, Yahweh upbraided the Israelites for rebelling against him. They had become

---

4. 2 Kgs 21:2–8.
5. Jer 44:17–18.

> A sinful nation, a people whose guilt is great, a brood of evildoers, children given to corruption! They have forsaken the LORD; they have spurned the Holy One of Israel and turned their backs on him. Why should you be beaten anymore? Why do you persist in rebellion? Your whole head is injured, your whole heart afflicted. From the sole of your foot to the top of your head there is no soundness—only wounds and welts and open sores, not cleansed or bandaged or soothed with olive oil.[6]

Jeremiah is remembered because of his fierce condemnations of the Israelites and his prophecies of destruction. "I will appoint over them four kinds of destroyers, says the LORD: the sword to slay, the dogs to tear, and the birds of the air and the beasts of the earth to devour and destroy. And I will make them a horror to all the kingdoms of the earth."[7] And, "Your wealth and your treasures I will give as plunder, without charge, because of all your sins throughout your country. I will enslave you to your enemies in a land you do not know."[8] And,

> "Your ancestors forsook me," declares the LORD, "and followed other gods and served and worshiped them. They forsook me and did not keep my law. But you have behaved more wickedly than your ancestors. See how all of you are following the stubbornness of your evil hearts instead of obeying me. So I will throw you out of this land into a land neither you nor your ancestors have known, and there you will serve other gods day and night."[9]

So offensive was the behavior of the Israelites that God forbade Jeremiah to pray for them. "Do not pray for the well-being of this people. Although they fast, I will not listen to their cry; though they offer burnt offerings and grain offerings, I will not accept them. Instead, I will destroy them with the sword, famine and plague."[10]

---

6. Isa 1:4–6.
7. Jer 15:3–4.
8. Jer 15:13–14a.
9. Jer 16:11–13a.
10. Jer 14:11b–12.

Walking Blind

The intent of the book of Chronicles (one book on two scrolls) was to document the apostasy of the Israelites. The book concludes with a severe condemnation of the Israelites, showing that Israel and Judah had earned Yahweh's wrath. "The Lord, the God of their ancestors, sent word to them through his messengers again and again, because he had pity on his people and on his dwelling place. But they mocked God's messengers, despised his words and scoffed at his prophets until the wrath of the Lord was aroused against his people and there was no remedy."[11]

In his disappointment and anger, God brought down both kingdoms. The northern kingdom of Israel fell first. Israel came under subjection to Assyrian invaders, and when the king of Israel rebelled, the Assyrians came into Israel, crushed the city of Samaria and forced the population to scatter into various localities in the Near East, and in their place they brought in gentiles from elsewhere to occupy the land (722 BC).[12] One hundred twenty years later the southern kingdom, Judah, was subdued by a Babylonian army (605 BC).

And even though the king of Judah, King Jehoiakim, had initially submitted to Babylonian control, he rebelled in 598 BC. That brought the Babylonians back to the city of Jerusalem where, after a short siege, displaced the king for his younger brother Zedekiah. But nine years, later Zedekiah brought about his own demise and the final humiliation of Jerusalem by rebelling against the Babylonians. Once again they returned, this time to besiege the city for eighteen months, leaving the city to starve. The poets who later recorded the experience in the city recorded its anguish: "Infants and babes faint in the streets of the city."[13] "Children faint for hunger at every street corner."[14] "Those who once ate delicacies are destitute in the streets. Those brought up in royal purple now lie on ash heaps."[15] Eventually

---

11. 2 Chr 36:15–16.
12. 2 Kgs 17.
13. Lam 2:11.
14. Lam 2:19.
15. Lam 4:5.

they would eat their offspring: "With their own hands compassionate women have cooked their own children."¹⁶

Finally, as the king fled the city, he was captured and obliged to witness the slaughter of his sons, and then he was deprived of his sight. He and the other nobility were carried off to Babylon while the poorest of the Jews were left to till the soil. Jerusalem was sacked and burned. The writer of Chronicles explains why such a calamity occurred:

> He brought up against them the king of the Babylonians, who killed their young men with the sword in the sanctuary, and did not spare young men or young women, the elderly or the infirm. God gave them all into the hands of Nebuchadnezzar. He carried to Babylon all the articles from the temple of God, both large and small, and the treasures of the Lord's temple and the treasures of the king and his officials. They set fire to God's temple and broke down the wall of Jerusalem; they burned all the palaces and destroyed everything of value there. He carried into exile to Babylon the remnant, who escaped from the sword, and they became servants to him and his successors until the kingdom of Persia came to power.¹⁷

A psalmist in horror wrote as if he had witnessed the Babylonian invasion of the city:

> O God, the nations have invaded your inheritance; they have defiled your holy temple, they have reduced Jerusalem to rubble. They have left the dead bodies of your servants as food for the birds of the sky, the flesh of your own people for the animals of the wild. They have poured out blood like water all around Jerusalem, and there is no one to bury the dead.¹⁸

Another psalmist wrote about the violation and wrecking of the temple:

---

16. Lam 4:10.
17. 2 Chr 36:17–20.
18. Ps 79:1–3.

Your foes roared in the place where you met with us; they set up their standards as signs. They behaved like men wielding axes to cut through a thicket of trees. They smashed all the carved paneling with their axes and hatchets. They burned your sanctuary to the ground; they defiled the dwelling place of your Name. They said in their hearts, "We will crush them completely!" They burned every place where God was worshiped in the land.[19]

PROMISES TO THE DEFEATED

It was in their exile that the Jews began to reflect on what had happened. It was then that they began to pay attention to what the prophets had been saying in previous times, when the bulk of the Israelites had spurned their warnings and admonitions. In their humiliation and defeat, the people of Judah began to internalize what they should have learned long before. Yahweh had said, through the pen of Isaiah, "If only you had paid attention to my commands, your peace would have been like a river, your well-being like the waves of the sea. Your descendants would have been like the sand, your children like its numberless grains; their name would never be blotted out nor destroyed from before me."[20]

Had they listened to the prophets, they would have avoided the horrors of the siege, the ruination of their city, and their exile to life under the Babylonians. They would have instead enjoyed God's favor. The Israelites had supposed that they had God's favor; they had supposed that they would be spared defeat because they were the custodians of Yahweh's temple; they had supposed that because his temple was in Jerusalem, he would not allow the city to fall.[21]

But they did not understand God's ways. They somehow felt they were beyond having to live by his standards; it was enough to invoke his name, to claim his favor because he dwelt in Jerusalem,

19. Ps 74:4–8.
20. Isa 48:18–19.
21. Jer 7:1–15.

their capital city. So, when the destruction came, and Jerusalem was destroyed and the temple burned, they were dismayed. They had been unable to grasp that God would allow his city and his temple, his dwelling place, built by Solomon at great expense and dedicated with such fanfare and solemnity, to be destroyed. They could not imagine how he could allow his people, descendants of the special friends of God, Abraham, Isaac, and Jacob, to be displaced from the land that God had given them. And they could not imagine how the city of God's servant David could have been violated by gentiles and be burned down and left a ruin. Their people had been conquerors, they had ruled all of Palestine: How could they now be so humiliated? Why were their lands taken from them by gentiles? Why had their children starved? Why were their women ravished?

These people had been looking back to their past, remembering past glories, without noticing that God had turned against them because they had in fact betrayed him in their way of life. They had been worshipping other gods. They had ignored his commandments. They had refused to listen to the prophets that had been sent to them. As a result, God had fostered the collapse of their world. Isaiah described them as "a people plundered and looted, all of them trapped in pits or hidden away in prisons. They have become plunder, with no one to rescue them; they have been made loot, with no one to say, 'Send them back.' . . . Who handed Jacob over to become loot, and Israel to the plunderers? Was it not the LORD against whom we have sinned? Or they would not follow his ways; they did not obey his law. So he poured out on them his burning anger, the violence of war. It enveloped them in flames, yet they did not understand; it consumed them, but they did not take it to heart."[22]

It was to these Israelites—defeated, humiliated, confused—that God made a particular promise: he would lead them through unfamiliar paths; he would make darkness light and rough places smooth; and he would by no means forsake them. The promise was composed for a people in confusion. And it was indeed in

22. Isa 42:22–25.

their confused state that the Israelites began to pay attention to what the prophets had been saying.

The book of Chronicles, in fact, appears to have been constructed to explain to the Israelites of a later time the reasons why God had brought them to such a pass. Likewise, the second section of Isaiah in which this promise appears, was written to encourage the Israelites through their most severe hours of trial. Isaiah 40 and following consists of a series of promises affirming that, even though the world of the Jews had been utterly wasted, God himself was alive and in control. He still had designs for them, which could be known if they would but redirect their attention to him and let him lead them through this difficult period.

This section of Isaiah is therefore rich in hope and promise; and it is filled with encouraging words for a people deprived of a sense of place and significance. That indeed is part of the appeal of our verse to me, for the promise to lead the blind in new paths, to make what is dark light, what is rough smooth, is not an abstract formulation for religious people who have always had their lives put together, who always made the right choices. Rather, it is for people who have known utter defeat, hopelessness, and ruined visions, and furthermore bear a sense of guilt for having betrayed God and so thwarted their best ambitions.

In particular, our verse is addressed to people whose faculties of perception have been blunted, who were foolish and unseeing, and now were quite lost. God reassures them that he has not forsaken them forever. They remain his people. "He who created you, Jacob, he who formed you, Israel: 'Do not fear, for I have redeemed you; I have summoned you by name; you are mine.'"[23] And, "This is what the Lord says—he who made you, who formed you in the womb, and who will help you: Do not be afraid, Jacob, my servant, Jeshurun [Upright One], whom I have chosen. For I will pour water on the thirsty land, and streams on the dry ground; I will pour out my Spirit on your offspring, and my blessing on your descendants."[24] And most notably, he promised to bring his people

23. Isa 43:1.
24. Isa 44:2–3.

back to their homeland. Yahweh says, "See, they will come from afar—some from the north, some from the west, some from the region of Aswan."[25]

Using Jerusalem to represent the dispersed and defeated exiles in Babylon the writer of chapter 49 of Isaiah offered a specific promise: "Lift up your eyes and look around; all your children gather and come to you. . . . Though you were ruined and made desolate and your land laid waste, now you will be too small for your people, and those who devoured you will be far away."[26] And he says, "Although you have been forsaken and hated . . . I will make you the everlasting pride and the joy of all generations. You will drink the milk of nations and be nursed at royal breasts. Then you will know that I, the LORD, am your Savior, your Redeemer, the Mighty One of Jacob."[27]

Such were the promises in which the Jews could take comfort collectively, as a whole. But some words of comfort in Isaiah were aimed at people forced to bear particular hardships. To those who would be herded across the desert and obliged to ford the rivers on foot, Yahweh said, "When you pass through the waters, I will be with you; and when you pass through the rivers, they will not sweep over you. When you walk through the fire, you will not be burned; the flames will not set you ablaze. For I am the Lord your God, the Holy One of Israel, your Savior."[28] To the ashamed and guilty Yahweh said, "I have swept away your offenses like a cloud, your sins like the morning mist. Return to me, for I have redeemed you."[29] To those who lacked hope and the strength to press on he said,

> Why do you complain, Jacob? Why do you say, Israel, "My way is hidden from the Lord; my cause is disregarded by my God"? Do you not know? Have you not heard? The LORD is the everlasting God, the Creator of the ends of the earth. He will not grow tired or weary,

---

25. Isa 49:12.
26. Isa 49:18–19.
27. Isa 60:15–16.
28. Isa 43:2–3.
29. Isa 44:23.

and his understanding no one can fathom. He gives strength to the weary and increases the power of the weak. Even youths grow tired and weary, and young men stumble and fall; but those who hope in the LORD will renew their strength. They will soar on wings like eagles; they will run and not grow weary, they will walk and not be faint."[30]

To the women who had lost their husbands or who could never marry because of the paucity of males, Yahweh said,

> Sing, barren woman, you who never bore a child; burst into song, shout for joy, you who were never in labor; because more are the children of the desolate woman than of her who has a husband. . . . Enlarge the place of your tent, stretch your tent curtains wide, do not hold back; lengthen your cords, strengthen your stakes. For you will spread out to the right and to the left; your descendants will dispossess nations and settle in their desolate cities. Do not be afraid; you will not be put to shame. Do not fear disgrace; you will not be humiliated. You will forget the shame of your youth and remember no more the reproach of your widowhood. For your Maker is your husband . . . the Holy One of Israel is your Redeemer.[31]

There was even a specific promise for men deprived of their sexual powers: "To the eunuchs who keep my Sabbaths, who choose what pleases me and hold fast to my covenant—to them I will give within my temple and its walls a memorial and a name better than sons and daughters; I will give them an everlasting name that will endure forever."[32] And of course there was, as we have noted, the promise to people who were blind: to lead them along paths unknown, to turn the darkness into light, to make crooked routes straight, and never to forsake them.

---

30. Isa 40:27–31.
31. Isa 54:1–5.
32. Isa 56:4–5.

CLAIMING THE PROMISE

Now, consider the requisite for this promise: you have to be blind. The promise was specifically addressed to the unseeing. Some, we have noted, were deliberately blinded by the Babylonians, but others would have been sightless for other reasons. The promise was given to them, and it would have been a basis for comfort for them as they were led off into a strange and alien land.

But the promise was of course intended for the people of Judah as a whole, for even the sighted felt lost, shaken and confused by the destruction of their society. This promise is for people who *feel* blind, as many Jews felt at this time. The world they had known had disappeared, as it were, without warning—for they had missed, even steadfastly ignored, all the signs. Now, far from their homeland, subjected to the dictates of barbarians, obliged to labor as menial servants for gentiles, the Jews had no hope of recovering the world they had known, or even of being buried with their ancestors.

Of course, this verse was preserved by a later generation that wanted to remember all that had happened and that in the kindness of God had become a source of understanding, wisdom, and comfort for later generations. It has been read and reread because it applies so well to the human condition: this is a promise for subsequent generations of people who have felt blind, who have had trouble sorting out the disorder, confusion, and calamities that befell them in their times. This is a promise for all of us when we cannot grasp what is happening, and dread what might be coming, when we cannot discern how to distinguish what the options before us are, when we are dismayed by the havoc that God has allowed.

I have felt this way at times and presume such confusion is familiar to others; I presume it to be a condition that most of us experience one time or another, possibly often. A well-educated young woman trapped in a humiliating situation once said to me, "I feel I am completely unequipped for the world I'm living in." The broad shifts in social worlds in recent years have deprived many people of a sense of how to prepare for the future. They are obliged to live from one day to the next, groping for anchorage—stability, certainty, security—in a world lacking fixed points. This is why God's promise to lead the blind along new tracks has meant so much to me. I have felt blind often—at least I have qualified for the promise!

Of course, there are lots of times when one feels assured of what's ahead and how to cope with it. But my experience has been that I am most apt to overlook what God wants me to notice when I am most confident. It is deceptively easy to behave like the Pharisees, who thought they had understanding but in fact missed the greatest revelation in history.[33] As Isaiah said, there is a seeing that doesn't perceive and a hearing that doesn't understand—conditions which the Pharisees' behavior well exemplified.[34] When Jesus wept over Jerusalem he exclaimed, "If you, even you, had only known on this day what would bring you peace—but now it is hidden from your eyes." They would be humiliated and Jerusalem would be wrecked, he said, "because you did not recognize the time of God's coming to you."[35]

It is possible to identify their failure, and then become guilty of it ourselves. We fail to recognize God's hand at work; we can suppose we see when we do not. That was the problem of the Laodicean church, who supposed they were rich, prosperous, and had no needs, ignorant that they were actually "wretched, pitiful, poor, *blind*, and naked."[36] The problem was not their wretchedness, pitiableness, poverty, blindness, and nakedness; we human beings are like that, in the eyes of God, according to Scripture. What was offensive to God was that the Laodiceans were oblivious to their actual condition. Supposing they were rich when they were destitute, they failed to offer the one requisite for God's favor—contrition, poverty of spirit—which would qualify them for God's blessing and acceptance.

The scriptural position is that a broken and contrite spirit is all we have to offer anyway. "'Heaven is my throne,' the Lord said

---

33. John 9:41.
34. Isa 6:10.
35. Luke 19:41–44.
36. Rev 3:17; emphasis added.

to them, 'and the earth is my footstool. Where is the house you will build for me? . . . [But]these are the ones I look on with favor: those who are humble and contrite in spirit, and who tremble at my word.'"[37] If the Bible is clear about anything, it is that the only thing you and I have to offer God is our wretchedness, our pitiableness, our poverty, our blindness, and our nakedness. And to such, who come to him with such poverty of spirit, affecting no claim of worthiness, he offers his cleansing, his inner renewing, his wealth, his sight, his covering. That is the point of his promise to lead us in new paths: it is a promise to those who know their blindness.

So to those who acknowledge an absence of clear sight, God promises to lead. The promise to the Israelites was that he would lead them in paths they had not known—certainly a challenge for the blind. It's the familiar pathways that are easiest for the blind, I presume; the sounds, perhaps the smells, can become familiar clues to one's location, so that one can get used to conditions along a well-known trajectory. But that was not in store for the Israelites. Not only were the people blind to whom this verse was directed, but they were also to be taken into strange places. No familiar clues would be given to which the Israelites could cue their expectations. They would all have to be led.

---

37. Isa 66:1–2.

2

The Walk of Faith

I suppose that for virtually everyone, life has its unpredictable turns. But a particular challenge of our times is that so much of the world around us is in the throes of continual and ever more rapid changes. The ground shifts beneath us; old certainties seem less sure now as unexpected situations arise and compound upon each other. The Scriptures aver that while God is the same yesterday, today, and forever our world could become radically caught up in crises that are beyond us. In any case, many passages in the Bible suggest that we human beings will always be struggling. And as individuals, we won't get it right—the life that pleases God, that is—without his help, without his guidance.

The Pharisaic tradition sought to develop a way to live that would honor the law as it should be honored, they thought. They devised a body of rules that they thought would ensure that they and their people would not, as had been the case before, stray from keeping God's law. This time they would do it right: they would keep the rules of "godliness." They would live by the law, carefully, strictly and precisely. And teach their people to do that also. The result was that, with attention fixed on the rules, they were unready to read God's will for them as the wider conditions of social life around them shifted. They did not see God at work to teach them and lead them in new paths as the ground under them kept shifting, requiring them to read not only the literal stipulations of the law but also the subtle implications of the law that needed to be appreciated in creative ways as the issues confronting them changed. Certain that they could see clearly how to live in the world, they became blind to what God wanted them in it. They had turned obedience to God into a carefully construed system of behaviors. With all the tenets of the system well worked out, they had no need, they supposed, to be open to God's personal concerns for their lives from situation to situation. They no longer had to keep working out ways to engage with the changing challenges before them, to engage with a lively God who was allowing new situations to test the authenticity of their devotion to him. God's intention was that they stay close to him. "As a belt is bound around the waist, so I bound all the people of Israel and all the people of Judah to me, declares the LORD, to be my people for my renown and praise and honor. But they have not listened."[1] To remain bound to him, they needed to be listening all the more closely to what their Scriptures could reveal for the immediate and changing problem of spiritual practice that life confronted them with.

THE WALK

Life with God is not a system but a walk, in which, through varying circumstances, we learn to watch for cues from him on how to behave in ways that honor him. We are to learn to seek his spiritual insights for the moment, for the immediate situation, which sometimes we have no preparation. It's not that rules are abolished or that the system in its broad outlines can be replaced; it's that the rules can never be sufficient. In real life the commands of God have to be applied creatively to new situations, one after another.

For the life of faith, one needs the counsel, leadership, and guidance of a living God who knows our problems, our pain, our

1. Jer 13:11.

humiliations and defeats. The life of faith cannot work without a meaningful sense of relationship to him. The spiritual walk can never be a system. It's a walk, often in uncertainty, or at least in unfamiliar settings, where the signposts are unclear, or are displayed, as it were, in an alien script. It is in the darkness that God promises to provide light and to make the crooked places straight, and in the rough places he will make things smooth. The central reality of a Christian walk is a God who is present with us, who understands, who sees our issues. The psalmist delights in God's engagement in his life: "I will be glad and rejoice in your love, for you saw my affliction and knew the anguish of my soul."[2] This God, who sees us in our depravity, knows how to lead and stabilize our inner selves as we traverse the darkness.

How to live through the rough times? God says, "I am the Lord your God, who teaches you what is best for you, who directs you in the way you should go," and he laments, "If only you had paid attention to my commands, your peace would have been like a river, your well-being like the waves of the sea."[3] His promise is to lead people who are dependent on him as sheep are on their shepherd: "They will feed beside the roads and find pasture on every barren hill. They will neither hunger nor thirst, nor will the desert heat or the sun beat down on them. He who has compassion on them will guide them and lead them beside springs of water."[4]

STEPPING INTO THE UNKNOWN

It is in the dark that we learn to trust in God. Promises to those who walk in the dark appear in the latter half of Isaiah, the chapters written to the Israelites for the confusion and despair they would experience during exile. The Lord, through Isaiah, challenged the Israelites, "Who among you fears the Lord and obeys the word of

2. Ps 31:7.
3. Isa 48:17–18.
4. Isa 49:9b–10.

his servant? Let the one who walks in the dark, who has no light, trust in the name of the LORD and rely on their God.[5]

The preeminent feature of the godly life is faith. Paul said, "For we live by faith, not by sight."[6] Indeed, he said, "I live by faith."[7] The faith that God calls us to is exercised in the confusion of life, in the interruptions and distractions. Real life is never as orderly as we think it ought to be. And yet it is in the discursiveness of life that God works. Jesus exercised his greatest impact in the distractions and interruptions. Beginning in chapter 9, verse 51, of the Gospel of Luke, the narrative is constructed as a series of interruptions as Jesus journeys to Jerusalem.[8] He was marching to his death. The tension builds as he travels southward from Galilee. Along the way he encounters people in need—a repentant tax collector, a blind beggar, a lawyer asking about the greatest commandment, and so on. In the interruptions, in the encounters that appeared to be distractions, Jesus demonstrated God's power and character to those around him.

In our lives, unwanted distractions and unforeseen events are occasions for discovering God's power, mercy, and love. That's how God intended us to live. Not that we should be disorganized, with no sense of direction, but that through the interruptions that seem to deflect us off course, through the encounters, surprises, and traumas of life, we might find help to see the hand of God and react in ways that display his character. That is the life of faith—being open to the new things he introduces into our lives, finding God in a dysfunctional world. Even—and especially—in the discursive affairs of life, God is at work. It is in the major disruptions of life that God promises to lead us.

His grace is addressed to those persons who are broken and shaken by failure, defeat, and loss. This God knows the anguish of your soul.[9] His grace is for people traumatized by unplanned

---

5. Isa 50:10.
6. 2 Cor 5:7.
7. Gal 2:20.
8. Luke 9:51—19:48.
9. Ps 31:7.

Walking Blind

failure, bereavement, hardship. In the verse I discussed in the first chapter, God says that even if you have been blinded—*especially* if you are sightless—he will lead you and help you through the turns of life. The person to whom God's promises are addressed is one who knows that he lacks clear vision as he faces an unpredictable world, one that seems unfamiliar and twisting. Micah lived well before the exile of the Judahites, but he foretold it and promised that they would be delivered precisely through such a traumatic experience: "You will go to Babylon; there you will be rescued. There the Lord will redeem you out of the hand of your enemies."[10] There—in Babylon, in the place of humiliation and defeat, of utter dismay, and confusion, where nothing is as it should be, where God seems to have abandoned his people to their deserts, even to worse than they deserve—there, the prophet says, you will be redeemed.

Prophesying at about the same time as Micah—that is, in the eighth century BC—Hosea, prophet to the northern kingdom of Israel, foresaw the destruction of their society because of their indifference to Yahweh, their god. Though painful, he said, that experience would purify them of their idolatry: "Therefore I am now going to allure her; I will lead her into the wilderness and speak tenderly to her. There I will give her back her vineyards, and will make the Valley of Achor [trouble] a door of hope. There she will respond as in the days of her youth, as in the day she came up out of Egypt."[11]

The exilic experience of the Israelites, cruel as it was, was a powerful vehicle of instruction. When the Jews returned to Jerusalem and Judah, they were religiously a different people. The uncertainty about their spiritual loyalties was gone. Never again would there be among the Israelites such a profligate worship of other gods. They learned, finally, through their suffering to have no other god besides Yahweh; there would never again be any doubt that he was the god of the Israelites; he it was that they would obey, for they had learned that he was a jealous god and would exact retribution for their sins.[12] From this lesson, of course, came their

10. Mic 4:10b.
11. Hos 2:14–15.
12. Exod 20:5.

attempts to formulate Yahweh's law into the elaborate system of rules that would become known as Pharisaism.

LISTENING IN FAITH

This brings us to another aspect of the life of faith. Looking for signs of God's will, listening for indications of how he will guide through the discursiveness of life: this is not a religious life. The promise that he would lead the blind in novel paths has nothing to do with religion. Religion is different from the life of faith. "Religion" refers to logically constructed formulations about God, truth, and virtue. Religion consists of coherently organized and persuasively argued systems of thought; it is structurally manifested in defined roles and statuses in the religious community, and behaviorally manifested in stylized forms of worship. Religion is organized and structured. The whole purpose of religion is to establish collective understandings, to standardize the forms of worship, and stipulate relations within the religious community. The religious life assumes predictability. The proper religious attitude seeks a way to deal with every situation, to develop in advance a moral reaction to every exigency.

The life of faith and obedience has other agendas and seeks the will of God from an entirely different viewpoint. It aims to conform to God's will in the discursive, unforeseen, unwanted developments of life. It entails, as the apostle Paul put it, sightless walking.[13] The believer, he said, should walk not by sight, but by faith in the One who has perfect vision and complete foresight, and has demonstrated his love for us. It entails trusting God, clinging to him in the interruptions that punctuate our lives, in circumstances not of our making, in challenges for which we feel unprepared and over which we have little control. The life of faith is essentially enabled by the help of God who is active and transcendent in our affairs. The believer knows that God's ways are higher than our ways; his purposes for his people are made known only in the broadest sense, so that his particular guidance for us,

---

13. 2 Cor 5:7.

in our specific circumstances, can never be fully anticipated. We seldom know where God is taking us in our spiritual journeys, but we come to know his presence and his enablement in the discursiveness of affairs, even in the heartbreaks, as life unfolds. In each new decision, each new relationship, each fresh encounter, there are possibilities for his guidance we may not have foreseen.

When Jesus called his disciples, he didn't give them much advance information to plan on. He simply said, "Follow me." What a turn of events for their lives his contact with them was! How radically he reshaped their lives and their experience! They were always only almost understanding what he was doing, what he was teaching them. Events outstripped the disciples' immediate ability to process what they were experiencing. They were often left to ponder what had just happened. And despite Jesus's specific predictions, they were quite unprepared for the abrupt and horrifying turn of affairs at the end of his life. They were terrified and dismayed by his capture, torture, and crucifixion. And despite his predictions, they were equally unready for his resurrection. Furthermore, when he spent time with them in the days after his resurrection, he gave them no clear notion of what to expect next. He left them no blueprint on how to continue the movement, how to start a church, not even directions on how to organize themselves. It was natural for them to want to know, before he departed from them, what would happen next. They asked, "Lord, are you at this time going to restore the kingdom to Israel?" His answer was, "It is not for you to know." Instead of a manual for the organization of a religious movement, he gave them a promise: "You shall receive power."[14]

Hardly had he ascended when they set about organizing. It was ordinary human behavior to concern themselves with structure: In choosing a replacement for Judas, they were performing a "religious" activity. Perhaps that act was useful, as far as the early Christian community was concerned. Matthias, who was chosen, was according to tradition a faithful witness of the teachings and works of Jesus. Indeed, reputedly, like all the others except John, he met a violent death for his witness. But we are able to see, from the

14. Acts 1:6–8.

vantage point of hindsight, that this simple act of the early apostles turned out to be of little note in the development of the church and the advance of the gospel.

As God's plan unfolded there were unforeseen turns of events—disappointments, victories, challenges, opportunities, disputes, gains for the gospel—the gospel expanded beyond the imagination of the small, timid cluster of followers had been left behind by Jesus. The community of believers expanded at least fiftyfold within a couple of months after Jesus's public humiliation and demise. Moreover, the church not only grew in numbers, but also in horizons. The persecution that followed the martyrdom of Stephen drove the church into non-Jewish communities. Within fifteen years, the ethnically diverse church at Antioch would be sending out missionaries to gentiles. But before this took place, the conversion of one of the church's most feared enemies, Saul (Paul), radically changed its fortunes. God was leading the community of early believers by a way they could never have foreseen, turning hopeless situations into dazzling victories, and intractable problems into opportunities, to build a new kind of institution, his church.

Through circumstances no one could have expected or imagined, God led and provided for the nascent community of believers who founded his church. He advanced his work through the capture and incarceration of Peter and John;[15] through the beating and threatening of the disciples;[16] through the stoning of Stephen;[17] through the persecution and dispersal of the disciples;[18] through the conversion and absorption of despised Samaritans into the community of believers;[19] and through the execution of James, the brother of John.[20]

---

15. Acts 4:1–4; 5:17–26.
16. Acts 5:40.
17. Acts 7:54–60.
18. Acts 8:1–8.
19. Acts 8:9–25.
20. Acts 12:1–2.

TRUSTING WHILE IN THE DARK

In a sense, there is nothing new here; it's the same message we find throughout Scripture: the life of faith—this trust in God even if one is led into uncharted waters—is the same sort of life God's faithful have always lived. They walked by faith. It is a life of trusting God in circumstances that seem beyond us, and impossible. We should not suppose that in earlier times the life of faith was easier. The men and women of faith who lived before us had to plough through the same cloud of confusion, doubt and short-sightedness that we do. Abraham was told to set out on a journey whose end and purpose he could not have known; God's real purposes would be revealed to him only as he moved, and then only to a measured degree; God's redemptive design is clearer to believers now than it ever was to him. Abraham was no more ready to live that way than we are. Yet through the experience of moving through, as it were, the darkness, the uncertainty, under the care and leadership of a God who clearly loved him, he came to know God as few have known him. The journeying, difficult as it must have been, was never the biggest problem: it was the strain of waiting. The promise, given in a private, intimate moment of revelation, had to be fulfilled. The French biologist Georges Buffon once defined genius as "a greater aptitude for patience."[21] Similarly, godliness is an aptitude for patience; it entails listening, watching, and waiting for God's signs, obeying what we truly believe to be his will, even when there is little result, when the outcome is unclear.

No better example of this kind of life exists in Scripture than Joseph. Despite his youthful sense that God was going to use him and do special things through him, he spent years in confinement, far from his family, with no hope of seeing them again, and no reasonable basis for supposing that the visions of his youth would ever be realized. He clearly felt isolated and abandoned for much of his adult life: "I was forcibly carried off from the land of the Hebrews, and even here I have done nothing to deserve being put in a dungeon." Clearly he longed for release: "When all goes well with you,

---

21. Buffon quoted in Séchelles, *Journey to Montbard*.

remember me and show me kindness; mention me to Pharaoh and get me out of this prison," he said to the chief butler.[22]

He had no choice about his condition: there were no avenues of escape. Joseph, one of the finest models of faith in Scripture, felt alone, abandoned, isolated. "How long, O LORD!"[23] the psalmist cried. But it is often here, in the context of loneliness and isolation that we come to appreciate the presence of God with us. Yes, who, indeed, "walks in darkness and has no light, yet trusts in the name of the LORD his God?"[24] Despite the humiliated detour in his life, Joseph escaped despair or bitterness that some of us would have nourished inside us. Joseph lived in the confidence that God was still sovereign in his world.

If the life of Moses is any indication, the life of faith can include disruption and the necessity to do what one feels unprepared for. Adopted into the wealth of Pharaoh's family, Moses's rash murder of an Egyptian to defend his people obliged him to flee the comforts he knew for an unfamiliar life in the desert. But in the land to which he had fled he was able to settle comfortably, taking a wife and fathering children. Then, when he was well ensconced in his new land, God intervened. He ordered Moses to abandon his comfortable life and return to Egypt. There, where he had been a marked man, he was to bring into being the liberation of his people, the Israelites, from their Egyptian taskmasters; he was to lead his people out of their bondage and into a land about which Moses knew nothing.

What a massive interruption that was! His responses to God's marvelous call exposed how deeply unready he was: he stalled ("Who shall I say you are?"); he protested ("They will not believe me"); he claimed incompetence ("O LORD, I am not eloquent . . . I am slow of speech"); finally, he pled, "Pardon your servant, LORD. Please send someone else."[25] God had interrupted at a most inconvenient time; moreover, the task God proposed entailed

22. Gen 40:14–15.
23. Ps 6:3 and many other places.
24. Isa 50:10.
25. Exod 3:13; 4:1, 10, 13.

great risk, and almost certain failure. The man we now regard as a supreme exemplar of godliness felt unready, unqualified, incapable of obeying God's call. It would have been easier to do something "religious"—to make a contribution, to piously encourage someone else to take up the challenge. God sees through superficial self-serving piety: he requires instead a more sincere faith, a more ready willingness to obey. Moses reluctantly gave God what he wanted: a willing, if tremulous, spirit.

The march of the Israelites through the wilderness under Moses's leadership was a fine example of the life of faith. Exodus tells us that they were led by a cloud by day and a flaming fire by night: "In all the travels of the Israelites, whenever the cloud lifted from above the tabernacle, they would set out; but if the cloud did not lift, they did not set out—until the day it lifted. So the cloud of the Lord was over the tabernacle by day, and fire was in the cloud by night, in the sight of all the Israelites during all their travels."[26] But before the Israelites could live that way, following the cloud or the fire dutifully, moving forward when it moved, staying put when it didn't, always without prior notice—before that Moses had himself been obliged to learn to live that way. He learned to follow and obey as God led and directed, without prior notice, with little preparation, little indication of what to expect next, armed with nothing more substantive than God's promise. The key element of this story was the reality of a real God actually leading them; it did not work through their own imagination.

We could go through Scripture considering how God called and led many of his servants in their weakness and how in unlikely situations, seemingly unprepared and unready, they faced new contexts where God could use them, where they could undertake tasks God had for them. David was called from the sheepfold to be anointed king of Israel;[27] Amos was called from dressing sycamore trees and tending sheep to denounce the spiritual decadence of Israel;[28] Jonah was called, indeed forced, to preach to Nineveh;

---

26. Exod 40:36–37.
27. 1 Sam 16.
28. Amos 7:14–15.

Nehemiah, the king's cupbearer, although more ready to undertake God's work than Jonah, could not have known what courage, dogged persistence, and zeal his task would require.

In New Testament times, the conversion of Saul, who became the apostle Paul, exceeded the imagination of the early disciples. Paul himself was stretched into projects that were unthinkable. "This man," the Spirit said to Ananias, "is my chosen instrument to proclaim my name to the Gentiles and their kings and to the people of Israel. I will show him how much he must suffer for my name."[29]

Paul, about whose life we know more than any of Jesus's disciples, was one of Scripture's richest examples of how a life of faith works in a diverse and changing world. He encountered hardships, setbacks, and numerous crises. To the Christians at Corinth he admitted that "we were under great pressure, far beyond our ability to endure, and we despaired of life itself, but that was to make us rely on God."[30] God was the secure anchor for Paul through years of conflict and suffering.

LIVING WITH UNCERTAINTY

God's promises have notable relevance for our times. It is a cliché now that the world is changing radically. People all over the world are facing new challenges, new situations, new opportunities. For some believers, the opportunities are legion; for others, the challenge is how to trust God in the midst of hardship, frustration, cruelty, and abuse. Some of us have to agonize over decisions that seem momentous. Every career decision, every job decision, every personal commitment becomes a struggle. We all crave certainty, a sense of what to expect. We worry that we miss the "best" possible option.

The making of decisions for young people can be agonizing. Many of us have looked for our lives as if they were hidden, a mystery. Years ago a friend of mine agonized about what she should

---

29. Acts 9:15.
30. 2 Cor 1:8.

take up as a career. She wanted to serve God. She struggled for many weeks, uncertain what she should do with her life, and in particular, what she should do next. Eventually, in her Scripture reading she encountered a verse from Isaiah: "Because the Sovereign Lord helps me, I will not be disgraced. Therefore have I set my face like flint, and I know I will not be put to shame. He who vindicates me is near."[31] The verse seemed to her an answer: if she cared so much about doing God's will, she wouldn't miss it. God was near and would not let her be disgraced. She could go on, make a decision that seemed right, trusting him to lead her, and if that wasn't the right course, he would redirect her toward what he wanted her to do. She took a step and was led, along a circuitous course she could never have envisioned, eventually to a position as director of one of the most influential organizations for young people in America.

God wants to lead us and enable us. The whole weight of Scripture is that, even though the future is unclear for all of us, God has plans for his people and provides grace for them through the uncertainties of life. Even when we mess up—and in my experience many of us will make mistakes that cause us deep shame and despair—even then God is ready to help us go on from wherever our failures have left us. If we are open to God's direction and provision, he will make his will known, in due time, as we step out, sometimes as if in the dark. It is possible to walk through the discursive events of life in a radically changing world with God as our friend and guide, along a course that makes our life a creative and distinctive representation of his unique character. Despite the turns we should not have made, despite the failures that mar his work through us, he is still with us, ready to redirect, enable, and guide. We have only to acknowledge our weaknesses, to learn to obey him as he leads us—sometimes in paths of which we are unfamiliar, even daunting. He enlightens the darkness and smooths out the rough places. And so we discover in our daily walk a sense of his glory and power.

---

31. Isa 50:7–8a.

3

Why I Believe in the Resurrection

He appeared to Cephas, and then to the Twelve... [and] to more than five hundred of the brothers and sisters at the same time,... [then] to James, then to all the apostles, and last of all he appeared to me.[1]

IT IS EASY TO challenge the claim of the early disciples that Jesus rose from the dead. But for that matter it is easy to challenge almost everything significant that the early Christians believed. The virgin birth? Jesus walked on water? Jesus raised people from the dead? The whole fabric of the Christian story is riven with claims of the impossible acts of Jesus. On the face of it anyone can doubt the claims made by the early disciples that Jesus did all these fantastic things. But of them all, the one that the early Christians considered decisive and irrefutable about Jesus—the assertion that he had come from outside the human spheres to declare a message for all humanity and to accomplish something of cosmic significance—was that Jesus had risen from the dead after being

---

1. 1 Cor 15:5–8.

publicly executed. This they proclaimed as the decisive evidence of his unique place in the history of human beings, and his distinctive importance in the plan of God for every human being. The resurrection claim is the one compelling challenge to credulity that everyone of us needs to face.

I went through a time when I questioned it, and I want to explain why I have come to certainty. I believe that Jesus of Nazareth rose from the dead, and I want to explain why. To do this I will examine three facts of history: the behavior of the Pharisees who had engineered Jesus's death and then opposed the story of his resurrection; the behavior of the disciples who at first disbelieved the story but then proclaimed it; and lastly, the behavior of Saul, later Paul, who began his career actively persecuting those who believed in the resurrection.

THE EVIDENCE OF THE PHARISEES

How did the Pharisees who opposed the resurrection give evidence of it? By what they didn't do.

During Jesus's life, the Pharisees had murmured against him for claiming that he could forgive sins. They had accused him of being the prince of devils when he healed a demoniac. They had opposed his performing miracles of healing on the Sabbath such as his healing someone burdened with "an unclean spirit," healing a woman who had long suffered continuous bleeding, and man who had dropsy. It seems like his curing of a man's withered hand on the Sabbath was the last straw. Those who saw it began to connive together how to destroy him.

A group of them tried to stone him to death for saying, "Before Abraham was born, I am!"[2] They abused him and insulted him, and insisted that he be crucified for his claim that "from now on you will see the Son of Man sitting at the right hand of the Mighty One and coming on the clouds of heaven."[3] And when

2. John 8:58.
3. Matt 26:64.

they finally saw him crucified they taunted him for claiming that he could "destroy this house," the temple, and raise it up in three days.[4] Moreover, once he was dead, they made sure that his corpse was kept under guard lest it disappear. For the Pharisees the body was important. They had heard that he had often predicted his rising on the third day after his death. They wanted to avert any shenanigans with the body, now that they had it, so the chief priests and Pharisees approached Pilate to ask him to secure the tomb of this "deceiver." Making sure that there would be no fraud, these leaders did everything which human prudence and cunning could foresee to protect the body. They set a military watch outside the tomb and placed an official seal on the entrance.

In view of all this, would the Pharisees conceivably have conspired to cause the body of Jesus to disappear? When the resurrection story came out, would they not have produced the body if they had it? All they had to do to stop the story once and for all was produce the body. But when Jesus's disciples began to preach his resurrection in the temple—they wouldn't stop teaching that Jesus was the Messiah, filling the whole city with this news—the Jews arrested them, questioned them, warned them, threatened them, and beat them. But they didn't do what they needed to do: produce the body. If Jesus was dead, where was the evidence? The time had come, the crucial moment for them to make an open show of the "fraud" of Jesus by presenting one final infallible evidence. Displayed to even a few witnesses, the corpse of Jesus would have settled the matter. That would reveal that the claim of his resurrection was false. There would be no "heresy" about a resurrection. And the claims of the apostles would be a joke. What came to be called the Christian "way" would never have existed. But the Pharisees produced no body. They didn't even claim to have the body. They didn't mention the body!

Something had happened that could not be explained. The body of Jesus, after it was placed in the tomb under guard, was gone. When Mary Magdalene came to the tomb early on Sunday

---

4. John 2:19.

morning she found the tomb open, the seal broken, and the stone rolled aside.

"They have taken the Lord out of the tomb," she said. "They have taken away my Lord!" When other women came to anoint his body, they also found no body, nor did Peter and John.[5]

The guards, after recovering from the shock of seeing a figure (an angel?) remove what must have been a huge stone, went to the chief priests and told them what they had seen—could they have heard of the resurrection earlier than anyone?—but even then these religious authorities failed to produce the body. They bribed the guards to say that the disciples had stolen the body while they slept.[6]

Strangely, they were lenient with the guards who had lost the crucial evidentiary proof against any and all claims of a resurrection. Did they really believe the corpse had been lost because of the guards' negligence? After planning his destruction for several months, finally carrying it out successfully, and then personally arranging for the security of the body, why didn't they demanded the guards be punished? (Roman practice was for them to be put to death.) In any case, why would they try to protect them? These same authorities would later beat the disciples for speaking of Christ's resurrection in the temple. Did they realize that the body had indeed mysteriously disappeared? Perhaps it had not been within the soldiers' power to keep the body.

THE EVIDENCE OF THE DISCIPLES' BEHAVIOR

But suppose there had been a series of bungles by the guards and even by the officials, couldn't the disciples somehow had been able to steal the body? The problem with this prospect is that their lives tell a different story. Their initial reaction to news of the resurrection was unbelief. But later they were convinced of it. They considered themselves ordained of God to be witnesses to it. Why should

---

5. John 20.

6. What would a lawyer do with this in court today? Who can say what happened while he slept?

such a change come over them, or why should they feel so strongly about what they knew was a lie?

On the first Easter morning when the women came with the news of the empty tomb it seemed an idle tale to the disciples. They didn't believe it. Even when they saw Jesus for themselves, they couldn't believe it. Although he showed them his hands and feet, they thought he was a ghost. Similarly, some people today suggest that Jesus's resurrection was spiritual, not physical. But Jesus was eager to dispel that idea among his disciples. "Look at my hands and my feet. It is I myself! Touch me and see; a ghost does not have flesh and bones, as you see I have."[7]

"Look," "touch," "see" were the words he used, for he wanted them to know that this was the same body which had been crucified. And while they still did not believe, he ate a piece of broiled fish from their table. If they were inclined afterward to wonder if they had seen a vision or had conjured their memory of him into a sense of his presence, they could remember that there was one less piece of fish on the table. His body was physical.

But Thomas was not present. The story of Jesus's appearance didn't convince him. What's more, he declared, "Unless I see the nail marks in his hands and put my finger where the nails were, and put my hand into his side, I will not believe." Later when the Lord appeared to Thomas, he said, "Put your finger here; see my hands. Reach out your hand and put it into my side. Stop doubting and believe."

"My Lord and my God!" was Thomas's awed acknowledgment of belief.[8]

Once they were convinced, the disciples considered themselves commissioned by God to testify to the resurrection. This was their high calling, their most pressing responsibility, their contribution to the world: to affirm the fact of his resurrection.

Seven times in the book of Acts they said they were witnesses to the resurrection. They set aside every menial task to allow full time to this ministry. They journeyed to the outskirts of the

---

7. Luke 24:39.
8. John 20:25–28.

then-known world, and many of them died violent deaths maintaining that they were witnesses to Jesus's resurrection.[9]

What fanatics they seemed to some! No clamoring social acclaim spurred them on to ignoble deaths. No upper room agreements could conceivably have induced them to preach and die for a lie. Surely they would have stopped short of this. Nor would moral maxims of their dead leader have inspired them to carry on the movement for which they knew he had died. Their deception would have sabotaged the movement. These men had been changed, they claimed, by an encounter with the living Savior. Certainly, one of the most convincing evidences for the resurrection was its effect on the apostles. Men who ran for their lives when he was betrayed, who watched him die from afar, who hid away in fear when he was buried: these men became fearless evangelists in the face of persecution, threats, even torturous deaths, once they had met the risen Christ.

The dark gloom of the cross was dispelled by unforgettable contact, they said, with a gloriously living person. To his death, Peter insisted that they were not following "cleverly devised stories" when they preached the power and coming of Jesus, but that they were "eyewitnesses of his majesty."[10] They had seen and heard and touched the risen Christ in the flesh. By their contact with Jesus, the risen One, they had no doubt: Jesus was alive. These twelve never gave up their confident declarations that Jesus had risen.

THE EVIDENCE OF A NOTABLE ENEMY

But did Jesus appear only to his followers? Why not to his enemies? Peter once said that Jesus was "not seen by all the people, but by witnesses whom God had already chosen—by us who ate and drank with him after he rose from the dead."[11] He showed himself to Mary Magdalene and the other women, to the two disciples who

---

9. Nelson, "How Did the Apostles."
10. 1 Pet 1:6.
11. Acts 10:41.

were walking toward Emmaus, to the apostles and to Peter and James individually, and to five hundred people who saw him at one time. He was seen alive for a period of forty days. But only by his followers.

Still, one person who didn't believe in him saw the risen Christ; a man notable for his unbelief, outstanding for his opposition to the Christian "way," famous for his intolerance of the resurrection witnesses: Saul of Tarsus.

Saul was an unlikely man to conjure Jesus back into existence, hardly one whose memory would ever quicken to a presence. He not only rejected the apostles' witness, he actively opposed it and was an accessory to the first murder of a Christian, Stephen. Adopting the pharisaical zeal that had crucified Jesus and stoned Stephen, he aimed to stamp out this heresy. He couldn't compromise with any part of it. It was evident in his behavior that the Christian claim that Jesus had risen—the whole Christian story— was a blight to the Jew, an insult to the law, rebellion from the God of his fathers. The claim that Jesus of Nazareth was God incarnate, risen from the dead, had to be quenched, brought to a quick end.

Twelve times the New Testament says that Saul persecuted the church. The long series of persecutions that continued through three centuries was aided in its beginning by this man, Saul of Tarsus. By his own testimony he violently abused Christians, abusing them in the synagogues and trying to force them to blaspheme, dragging them from their homes into prison.

He traveled to Damascus to quench the Christian movement there, possibly a journey of almost a week. But as they neared Damascus he and his friends were struck to the ground by a sudden light from heaven. A voice asked, "Saul, Saul, why do you persecute me?" "Who are you, Lord?" Saul asked. The voice replied, "I am Jesus, whom you are persecuting." At this moment Saul was confronted with the risen Jesus. He was given a message: "The God of our ancestors has chosen you to know his will and to see the Righteous One and to hear words from his mouth. You will be his witness to all people of what you have seen and heard."[12] "See,"

12. Acts 22:6–14.

"hear"—these words appear again in the Biblical record. And by what he saw and heard, the outstanding persecutor of the early church became a witness of the risen Christ to the world.

His life was reversed. The destroyer of the Christian faith became its defender; a participant in the murder of Stephen became a promoter of the gospel. The persecutor became a sufferer for the story he had persecuted. For the cause of Christ he endured mobs, beatings, imprisonments, perilous journeys, danger and physical affliction. Often near death, he received the Jews' thirty-nine lashes five times, was beaten with rods three times, was stoned and left for dead once, was shipwrecked three times and adrift at sea for several hours.

In his frequent journeys he faced dangers of many sorts: river crossings, bandits, and personal enemies who followed him from town to town. He lived a life of hardship and labor, working for a living with his hands. He experienced many sleepless nights, hunger, thirst, homelessness, frigid temperatures, exposure. He described his life as a spectacle, an exhibition of weakness. He was generally held in disrepute, considered a fool for Christ, treated as the scum of the world—all this to the end that the risen Christ be proclaimed to ever greater numbers of people. But even then, his experience of being was reviled, slandered, treated as an impostor, ignored by some, punished by others, held in disrepute by many, his heaviest burden, he said, was his anguish for his unbelieving Jewish brethren and the spiritual welfare of the nascent Christian community. Yet paradoxically, despite his sorrows, he rejoiced throughout his life at the privilege of serving Jesus, the risen One whom he had encountered near Damascus.[13]

Paul's sudden encounter with Jesus is the key to understanding his life. No epileptic seizure at Damascus, no sudden dawning of truth upon him, no resolution to stop his hateful razing of the church produced such a focused life. The change came from a unique encounter with the risen Jesus, described in the New Testament writings as the living One who was dead and is alive forever

---

13. The above paragraphs are a précis of 2 Cor 6 and 11.

by the power of an indestructible life.[14] When he met the risen Lord, the self-confessed chief of sinners, the most notorious persecutor of Christians, was transformed into a bond slave of Jesus. Throughout the rest of his life, Paul would proclaim that the unjust murder of Jesus and his resurrection from death were God's means of bringing about mercy, forgiveness, and salvation to the people of the world.

THE CONCLUSION

Three historical events—the failure of the Pharisees and the chief priests to keep track of the body of Jesus after his death, the fear and initial unbelief of the disciples who later at great risk would declare that Jesus had risen, and the transformation of Saul the anti-Christian into Paul the zealous apostle of Christ's resurrection—these events together reveal that Jesus Christ rose from the dead.[15]

---

14. Heb 7:16.
15. An early version of this chapter appeared in *HIS Magazine*, April, 1960.

4

Legal Certainty, Ethical Cowardice

THE CHALLENGE

I HERE EXAMINE A situation created by a group of religious experts who presented Jesus with a problem that they thought would challenge and embarrass him. Here is the story as it is told in the Gospel of John:

> At dawn he appeared again in the temple courts, where all the people gathered around him, and he sat down to teach them. The teachers of the law and the Pharisees brought in a woman caught in adultery. They made her stand before the group and said to Jesus, "Teacher, this woman was caught in the act of adultery. In the Law Moses commanded us to stone such women. Now what do you say?" They were using this question as a trap, in order to have a basis for accusing him.
> But Jesus bent down and started to write on the ground with his finger. When they kept on questioning him, he straightened up and said to them, "Let any one of you who is without sin be the first to throw a stone at her." Again he stooped down and wrote on the ground.

At this, those who heard began to go away one at a time, the older ones first, until only Jesus was left, with the woman still standing there. Jesus straightened up and asked her, "Woman, where are they? Has no one condemned you?"

"No one, sir," she said.[1]

PROVENANCE QUESTIONS

One issue of interest before I examine this story is its peculiar provenance. In the early manuscripts this incident in the life of Jesus is told in different places in the Gospel of John. In some it appears in chapter 8 (vv. 1–11); in others in chapter 21 (just before the closing sentence). Also, it appears in a few early manuscripts of the Gospel of Luke (at the end of chapter 21). And in some of the earliest manuscripts of either Gospel it does not appear at all.

So, was there some kind of issue with this story? Could it have been written by John and then left out by mistake? It doesn't look like the kind of mistake a copier would make. Could it have been written by someone else and inserted into one of these two Gospels? Why does it even appear in the manuscript of another Gospel? Could it have been deliberately left out of some manuscripts? It seems to have been one of those incidents in the life of Jesus that was noted down early by the disciples, and collected into an early body of stories about Jesus from which the Gospel writers drew as they put together their respective presentations for their particular audiences. Is there something about this story that relates to the characters in it? Did the problem have to do with what happened after this event? Something about the woman? I will return to this question after examining some interesting details in the incident described here.

---

1. John 8:2–11.

THE SCENE

In any case, the story in question has a distinctive appeal for the focus is on a woman who has been caught in a compromising situation and is now being presented to Jesus in the temple as a crowd gathers to see what is going on. Her plight draws us into the story. We wonder about her: who is she? How was she apprehended? What was the relationship of these religious authorities to her? How did they know she was having illicit sex with someone? We would like to know more about her and how she came to be here. What was her story? Of course, there is a glaring omission of her consort in the affair. Where is he? Why was he not brought with her? And at the end of the story we want to know what happened next: what happened to the woman?

The setting was one that was probably common: Jesus was teaching in the temple, presumably in the portico, the open pavement outside the entrance to the temple, and a group of followers were there listening; possibly some of them had even come to the temple to hear him teach. On this particular morning he was interrupted by a few experts in religious law who presented to him a woman whom they said had been "caught in the act of adultery." And they have a question for Jesus. They remind him that Moses decreed that such a person must be stoned to death, and they want him to declare his own opinion, whether she should be executed as the law stipulates, or not. They asked him, "What do you say?"

The text says that they did this "to test him." So the whole episode was a setup. This woman had been caught having sex with someone who has been carefully protected from accusation whereas she was exposed in the public place in order to test Jesus. According to the text they wanted to trap him so "that they might have some charge to bring against Jesus." They were accusing the woman in order to accuse Jesus.

The appearance of these scholars of the law and their captive woman has reshaped the scene. There are now two circles of people in the portico of the temple, an outermost circle composed of the onlookers who had come to hear Jesus teach but have now

Legal Certainty, Ethical Cowardice

gathered around with great interest in this interruption. And there is an inner circle composed of the legalists presenting Jesus with a kind of challenge, and at the center of this clamorous inner circle, is a woman, standing alone. I wonder how she was dressed, as she seems to have been forced to leave abruptly, with little time to prepare. She must have complained as she was being dragged away but now, in public, humiliated, she is silent. The crassness of her plight is manifest: she appears before this crowd in a most compromising, embarrassing pose. Everything about the moment seems callous if we have any feelings for this woman. She is clearly helpless. No one rises to defend her. This is a man's world, and this vulnerable, helpless, humiliated woman is a pawn in it.

Such is the scene. But what is left unsaid is important. This little cabal of legal experts has hatched a scheme to embarrass the young rabbi, Jesus of Nazareth, on a point of law. And why? Was it that he was more popular than them? They are posing an awkward problem to him—the adultery of this woman—in order to prompt him to say something that can be used against him. Whatever actually happens to her—whether she is stoned to death or not—seems to be of little interest to them. But they are doing this without revealing anything about her consort, also discovered in the act. His absence makes their project seem awkward, contrived. It reveals that this is a charade. And the woman is a mere prop in a scheme hatched merely to pose an awkward legal problem to a too-popular rabbi.

JESUS SHIFTS THE FOCUS

At the same time, as the legalists are pressing Jesus for an answer, he is paying no attention to them. He is busy writing on the ground, drawing words in the sand, I presume, marks that will soon vanish, blown away by the morning breeze. But what is he writing? We are never told. In any case, the accusers are paying no attention to him, at least at first. They are fixed on forcing him to respond to the issue they have posed. Then Jesus stands up, looks directly at the accusers, and says, for everyone to hear, "Let him who is without sin cast the first stone." Now the accusers take notice of what he has been doing.

What he said seems to have silenced the clamor. The accusers are taking in what Jesus has said. He has invited one of them, the most pure of them, the most renowned for his upright life, to step forward and throw the first stone. And he returns to writing in the sand. Now what he is writing has the attention of everyone. Everyone stretches to see the words that he is carving in the sand. They also are watching for who will step forward and throw the first stone. Will anyone declare himself worthy—without sin—by stepping forward? There is an awkward silence.

No one steps forward.

Why? Up to this moment the accusers have been part of a group. Each member of the clamoring knot of legal authorities was a part of the whole. But for one of them to step forward, an act for everyone to see, would be to declare himself distinct among his colleagues, spiritually pure enough to take the lead. In fact, these religious authorities were known to many, each one of them. People there knew them. Was any of them "without sin"? The folks looking on would have had their own opinions about that.

Mob behavior is strange in that the individuals who collectively compose a mob do things they later do not want to own. They can later be ashamed of what they did as part of a collectivity. The French sociologist Émile Durkheim was impressed by this phenomenon. He wrote, "The great movements of enthusiasm, indignation, and pity in a crowd do not originate in any one of the particular individual's consciousnesses. They come to each one from without and can carry us away in spite of ourselves. . . . Once the crowd has dispersed, that is, once these social influences have ceased to act upon us and we are alone again, the motions which have passed through the mind appear strange to us, and we no longer recognize them as ours. It may even happen that they horrify us, so much were they contrary to our nature."[2] Durkheim is here saying that in a crowd, an individual may not behave as he normally would elsewhere. In a crowd each individual tends

2. Durkheim, "Social Fact," 87.

to behave as part of an anonymous collectivity, and so recognizes no personal responsibility. Crowd anonymity allows people to do things they would not do as individuals.

These scribes and Pharisees came to Jesus as a group, as a kind of social bloc, presenting themselves as united in the scheme they had hatched. And as a bloc they were acting together. But Jesus's invitation shifted the nature of the situation: He had called for one of them—any one of them—to act as an individual while the rest were looking on. In this case, those who watched became judges of whoever would step forward. That person in this case would not be anonymous. He could not throw the first stone without being identified as a specific individual.

This seems to be the way the accusers assessed the new situation, for each of the accusers slipped away, one by one, "beginning with the eldest." What began as a scheme to challenge Jesus became a threat to the eminent authorities who were accusing the woman, as none of them was anonymous. The most eminent among them slipped away first. Then another, then another. One by one—in rank order—the accusers left.

JESUS AND THE WOMAN ALONE

Now, finally, "Jesus was left alone with the woman standing before him." We wonder if exactly no one was left to observe what happened next. Could even the onlookers, the gawkers, have also tiptoed away—embarrassed to be participants in the heartless exposure of this defenseless woman? In any case, there was now no mob.

This seems to have been the first time that Jesus and the woman actually made eye contact. Jesus has spent most of the time facing the ground, until this instant. He looks up and asks the woman, "Where are they? Has no one condemned you?" "No one," she says. Jesus responds, "Neither do I condemn you. Go, and sin no more."

This was his response to the challenge that the accusers had posed for him. He chose to show her mercy. It is possible that the accusers already expected that Jesus would want to let her go, and this was the trap they had posed for him: By showing mercy he would then be disobeying the law. In any case, none of the accusers were present to use his response against him.

QUESTIONS REMAINING

The omissions in this story still trouble us. We don't know who the woman was. Or who her paramour was. Or why he was not present. Or why he was never mentioned. Also, we have no clear sense of what Jesus wrote in the sand. We are left to wonder about some titillating details.

Even so, this story was preserved for a reason. The Gospel writer—at least someone who wanted the story told—wanted us to draw something interesting about Jesus, even if they didn't want to reveal some of the most interesting details. I of course have no answers to my questions, but I believe the ambiguities and omissions in the story are intentional. The author is calling upon us readers to construct a lesson about what this event teaches us while hiding certain details for reasons of their own.

So, I here venture a construction of my own on a few of the missing details, especially with regard to the woman. She had been caught committing a forbidden act. She had been treated roughly, publicly exposed and humiliated, displayed as a "sinner" for the public to see, and brought to the brink of almost certain public execution. But then she was abruptly released, able to walk away from the whole ordeal uncondemned. What would this whiplash of abrupt and radical shifts in her status have done to her? How did she react to her release from all charges? And what might she have done with her life thereafter? And what did Jesus mean to her now?

Jesus's last words to the woman, "Neither do I condemn you. Go and sin no more," may be a clue to what happened to her, or rather, how she responded to the reprieve he had given her. Could she in fact have repented of her sin? What did she do now? It is easy to surmise that she had responded with joy, moreover, to demonstrate her gratitude for what had done for her. Wouldn't she have been forever grateful for his kindness? Would she not have desired earnestly to please him? To live out her life as he had directed her? He had saved her from her accusers, spared her life, declined to condemn her, even though she knew, and he knew, and the crowd knew, as well as her accusers, that she was guilty as charged. Jesus's only comment to her had been his directive to "sin no more." He had saved her from death, even from public condemnation and execution, and enjoined her only to "sin no more." Was this not the defining moment of this woman's life? Surely, she realized that she owed Jesus everything. Every breath. Every moment of the rest of her life.

Could she have become a faithful follower of Jesus and joined the community of Jesus's followers? If so, maybe this was the reason the author of the text left out so much of the story. In fact, would this story have been worth telling if the woman had rejected Jesus's admonition and gone back into a life of "sin"? It is no leap of imagination to surmise that this woman became a member of the newly forming community of believers, perhaps even a notable figure in it. In such a case it would have been courteous for whoever told the story to conceal her identity.

Even so, the author who put down this account wanted his readers to know about the whole affair because it revealed something significant about Jesus—namely, that he was gracious to sinners, showed mercy to the defenseless and humiliated. This is a story about mercy. Especially redemptive mercy—that is, mercy that transforms lives. If indeed the woman embraced the mercy accorded her, to repent of her sins and commit herself to following Jesus, seeking to please the one who had saved her, then this is a story of how Jesus through his mercy transformed a life. She was an exhibit of what a generous, open-hearted, compassionate person could do for a sinner. This woman was free to renounce any claims Jesus had on her, to reject his appeal to "sin no more." But the shock of her deliverance from almost certain death must have profoundly touched her and created in her a desire to fulfill all that Jesus asked of her. The man who had saved her, freed her, and refused to condemn her had asked her to turn away from adultery. How eagerly would she have embraced his request! How earnestly would she have desired to fulfill all that he asked of her! Having been given life, was she not now indebted to him for life? The life she would live thereafter, would it not be for him?

This indeed is what we mean by gospel, the good news that Jesus has offered us mercy and called upon us to renounce our sins and live out the life of service, ministry, forgiveness, and generosity that he displayed in this community. This is what it means to embrace the mercy accorded us through Jesus. He, the Gospel announces, paid the debts of shame and punishment we all deserve, paying for all the debts before God that we have incurred, fulfilled all the obligations we could not fulfill, so that we can live out, from our hearts, the love and mercy that we have received from him. Can we do anything other than sincerely seek to live lives that please him?[3]

In fact, this woman is an image of all of us. We are all guilty before God; we all deserve punishment for our sins; none of us is free from guilt. And yet, Jesus by taking upon the sin of the world bore the wrath of God in our behalf. This is how we understand the hideous brutality of Jesus's crucifixion. It was more than the death of an innocent man. It was a material enactment of the cosmic act of atonement for the sin of us unworthy sinners. This is how we understand the resurrection of Jesus from the dead: as an announcement that our sins have been paid for. Our obligations before God have been completely fulfilled, so that we can go free to "sin no more," to live out new lives that demonstrate our gratitude, seeking to display the gracious character of Jesus in the world. We are called to live to please him who has shown to us mercy. It was mercy that we did not deserve, mercy that we did not earn, mercy that has expunged all our debts, all our shame, all our sins.

---

3. 2 Cor 5:15.

5

Biblical Advice on Nonreligious Living

Carry each other's burdens, and in this way
you will fulfill the law of Christ.[1]

IT IS CUSTOMARY FOR us to say that Jesus was a great religious teacher. But in some ways, Jesus's teaching was not very religious. For most of us, the word "religion" implies rituals, dogmas, icons, images aimed at relating to God or at least to unseen spiritual forces. Saying prayers, celebrating fasts, reciting incantations or special formulas, genuflecting, and other acts of submission, etc.

Jesus's teachings were not "religious" in that sense. And for that reason he often clashed with the religious officials of his day. He allowed his disciples to shuck and eat grains of wheat on the Sabbath day whereas the religious leaders had declared that no one should do such "work" on the sacred day. Jesus criticized the way

---

1. Gal 6:2.

that some pious people performed their religion for others to see. "And when you pray, do not be like the hypocrites, for they love to pray standing in the synagogues and on the street corners to be seen by others. Truly I tell you, they have received their reward in full. But when you pray, go into your room, close the door and pray to your Father, who is unseen. Then your Father, who sees what is done in secret, will reward you."[2] Similarly, he taught his disciples that they should not parade the giving of alms. "When you give to the needy, do not let your left hand know what your right hand is doing," he said.[3]

For Jesus, true faith was a matter of the heart—that is, what goes on within our inner private selves.[4] And he accosted religious leaders with the critical assessment of Isaiah: "These people come near to me with their mouth and honor me with their lips, but their hearts are far from me. Their worship of me is based on merely human rules they have been taught."[5]

Yes, true faith inside the self is what God honors, he said. Such a concept is so contrary to what some people think religion is that it is not easy to explain. One time I was in a conversation with some people in another country where Christianity was not freely practiced. It was winter and we were sitting on a wooden floor around a wood stove talking about religion.

They were curious about me. They supposed I was a Christian and they asked me about my faith. One person in particular, a truck driver, was especially eager to know what my obligations were as a Christian. I explained as I best could in that setting and in their language, that the obligation of Christians is to love God with all their heart, soul and mind, and to love their neighbors as themselves. (This is the way I read the Scripture; I know other people would say something else.) We have this obligation, I explained, because Christ died on the cross to pay for our sins before God.

---

2. Matt 6:5–6.

3. Matt 6:3.

4. This, in fact, is the teaching throughout Scripture. It is specifically argued by Paul in Rom 3.

5. Isa 29:13.

His death was a sacrifice that cleanses us before God so that he can accept us, show us mercy and love, despite our unworthiness. What was required now was to accept his gift of salvation through Christ and then to show our gratitude by loving him, keeping his commandments, and loving our neighbors. Beyond this we have no special things to do because Christ's death did it all for us. His death was the supreme ritual that he performed for us. All this I explained as I best could. The truck driver listened carefully, but he found it difficult to grasp what I was saying. "You have nothing to do?" he asked. "What do you have to do?" I went through my explanation again. To that he said again, "But what do you have to do?" He continued to be confused. Finally, one of his friends broke in and, in effect, said, "Look, numbskull, he's saying that the debts are paid. All you have to do is receive his salvation as a gift!" The trucker turned to me and with tears in his eyes said, "We can never know. We can never be sure."

The notion that faith is essentially a matter of the heart can leave some people with the impression that in Christianity there are no rules. Once I was attending a reception at an embassy in a capital city of a Muslim country. That country had severe rules against drinking alcohol but this was a reception for foreign diplomats: alcohol was being served as a courtesy to the visitors. As I was visiting with some folks a high official of the host country came over and said to me with a smile, "I have become a Christian." This was a startling thing to say in a country that could put people to death for becoming a Christian. (I have known two people from that country who were killed for their faith in Christ.) This official was declaring to us that he had become a Christian. And he was smiling. It took a moment to catch his point. In fact, he was jesting. It was a kind of confusing joke. He was holding a glass of gin and took that to be a sign of what Christians do. Apparently for him being Christian meant being free to drink alcohol. It has been easy for some of my friends to suppose that there are no rules in Christianity: no rules against alcohol, no dietary rules—and no rules against the most egregious human vices? Such suppositions are of course gross misunderstandings of the religion that grew out from Jesus's teaching. No, that's not what Jesus taught.

But if there are obligations, what are they? Is there nothing to say about what we have to do? How should we behave if we want to please God? Is it not obvious that Christianity should have at least some directives for life? A religion should at least provide guidance on how to please the deity we worship.

Jesus's teaching on how to live comes out in a discussion he had with a specialist in the Mosaic law. It was initiated by a question that the jurist posed in order to test Jesus's grasp of the law. He asked him,

> "Teacher," he asked, "what must I do to inherit eternal life?"
>
> "What is written in the Law?" he replied. "How do you read it?"
>
> He answered, "'Love the Lord your God with all your heart and with all your soul and with all your strength and with all your mind;' and, 'Love your neighbor as yourself.'"
>
> "You have answered correctly," Jesus replied. "Do this and you will live."
>
> But he wanted to justify himself, so he asked Jesus, "And who is my neighbor?"
>
> In reply Jesus said, "A man was going down from Jerusalem to Jericho, when he was attacked by robbers. They stripped him of his clothes, beat him and went away, leaving him half dead. A priest happened to be going down the same road, and when he saw the man, he passed by on the other side. So too, a Levite, when he came to the place and saw him, passed by on the other side. But a Samaritan, as he traveled, came where the man was; and when he saw him, he took pity on him. He went to him and bandaged his wounds, pouring on oil and wine. Then he put the man on his own donkey, brought him to an inn and took care of him. The next day he took out two denarii and gave them to the innkeeper. 'Look after him,' he said, 'and when I return, I will reimburse you for any extra expense you may have.'"

"Which of these three do you think was a neighbor to the man who fell into the hands of robbers?"

The expert in the law replied, "The one who had mercy on him."

Jesus told him, "Go and do likewise."[6]

Consider the nature of this interchange. Here is a jurist, a specialist in interpreting the religious law, who was dubious of Jesus, and he asked a question to test him, "What must I do to inherit eternal life?" In legal discussion, issues like this are examined in the abstract: rational discourse is crucial to legal thought and argumentation. So, it is safe to surmise, and the jurist's reaction later bears this out, that his question was to test Jesus's judicial knowledge and analytical acumen: how would he identify, and make a case for how one gains eternal life?

When Jesus asked for his own judgment on the question the jurist seemed ready enough; indeed, he recited verbatim the relevant texts in the law (with a slight augmentation).[7] It is easy to picture a learned man here answering with a degree of pride, eager to display his erudition. And erudite he indeed was, and for that Jesus commended him.

Jesus drew out of this legal expert the answer to his own question as it was posed, "What should he do to inherit eternal life?" The answer was to love God with heart, soul, strength, and mind and to love his neighbor as himself. "Do this," Jesus says, "and you will live."

Stated this way, the issue was no longer a matter of abstract analysis: it was now a matter of doing something to live out in practice. How indeed shall any of us love God with all our hearts, souls, strength, and minds, and also love our neighbors as ourselves? The jurist already knew the answer. The problem, for him, and for us—which Jesus's response implicitly pointed out—was how actually to do that.

---

6. Luke 10:25–37.

7. The order "Love your neighbor as yourself" is not in the Ten Commandments. It appears in Lev 19:18.

This simple reply by Jesus, with presumably others standing by, placed the jurist on the defensive. So, he ducked into a juristic quibble, "Who is my neighbor?" With this answer he was saying, in effect, "Let us parse the wording of this commandment more exactly so that we can specify all the conditions, all the particulars, by which the commandment is to be fulfilled."

Loving God is sufficiently abstract a concept that people can claim to be doing it without contradiction because it cannot be seen. (It is often claimed by officials who want public acclamation.) But loving your neighbor belongs to a different order of reality altogether: it is a matter of behaving in the presence of others who can have their own opinions of our behavior.

What began with an opportunity to display erudition in the subtleties of the law now became a search for specificity. But Jesus did not answer the jurist's question directly. Instead, he told a story. I wonder, did the event he described really happen? Or was the story a kind of parable? Or a hypothetical? In the end, the story would shift the focus from who is our neighbor to how to be a good neighbor.

Note some significant features of the story.

First, all three of the travelers saw this pathetic figure at the side of the road. And all of them recognized that this person needed help.

Second, the way they behaved displayed how disposed they were to recognize an obligation to help him. The circumstance before them forced them to respond to what they saw. They had to ignore the bleeding man and "pass by on the other side," or they had to interrupt their travel plans and help him. And what helping him could mean was unclear. It would take time. It could require money. There was no telling what else might be required. And besides, all this would be for a total stranger.

Third, this whole episode happened by chance. Obviously, the travelers had not expected to face such a situation. How they acted in this moment revealed how disposed they were to recognize any obligation to this stranger. The challenge presented by the situation was how to decide in the moment what to do.

In life we are often waylaid by unforeseen events. And the way we react reveals how disposed we are to adjust to a different reality than we had planned on. The rule to love our neighbors is less a particular thing to do than a disposition to bring to every moment. Without being disposed to love people, to help when a person's need appears before us without warning, we are unlikely to respond with immediacy and effectiveness. I confess that I have been unready to be generous and gracious at times when I was faced with a major interruption in my plans. By chance the victim had suffered the abuse of thieves and by chance the three travelers had come upon his miserable condition. Their response revealed how disposed they were to behave in the interest of someone besides themselves.

The problem with the command to love our neighbors is that it doesn't tell us what to do. There are no guidelines. No religious ways or times to do it. Instead, it requires a readiness to help, to invent a response that is appropriate to a helpless person in need. The traveler had to figure out what to do—in that instant, in that situation. The actions required in loving our neighbor cannot be specified. They have to be invented on the spot, in the moment according to the situation.

Loving others demands creativity. I learned this from my wife Rita. She showed love for our neighbors in ways that I would never have dreamed of. Her loving acts of friendship and kindness to our neighbors came out of who she was. What she did was natural to her. I realized, watching her, that loving someone as Jesus taught us to love requires creative thought. What we do, of course comes from what is inside us. The way we love our neighbor, what we do, has to be invented. We have to assess the situation and act accordingly, to show kindness, to be a friend, to love. If I am to love people at all I have to be creative.

This rule—in fact, all the religious duties that Jesus taught—requires, to repeat myself, that we bring to every moment, to every situation, a disposition to act in the interests of others. We must be ready to see the needs of others and to act in support of them, in their situation. In fact, this readiness to act in the interests of others is already modeled for us in the way God has loved us: "While we were yet sinners Christ died for us," says Paul.[8] We are to display to those around us the generous, open-hearted character of the God who saved us. In the way he has behaved toward us we are to behave toward others. The love that reached out to me and invited me to embrace his mercy is the love that I want to be prepared to show to everyone I encounter. Such are the rules of Christ. This is why Paul could tell the Galatians with confidence that fulfilling the law of Christ meant bearing each other's burdens.[9]

But there is another side to this. Whatever we do and say will be judged. "Everyone will have to give account on the day of judgment for every empty word they have spoken. For by your words you will be acquitted, and by your words you will be condemned."[10] Yes, our words. Our words can reveal how disposed we are toward the interests of others.

So, if I am to "do" what Jesus taught his followers to do, I have to be disposed to act in the interests of others as situations arise, for I will be judged for the disposition to love, to show mercy, kindness, that I bring to every situation. Under the gaze of an all-seeing God I am to be disposed to love my neighbors creatively according to the circumstantial necessities of every moment. So, there are indeed rules for me as a Christian, but most of them cannot be specified. At the same time whatever I do will be judged.

No wonder it is difficult to grasp the obligations of the Christian before God! That's why Jesus's story is so useful: it succinctly and pointedly identifies how critical it is to improvise as we live out his commandments in practice.

Notice also how the story Jesus told coerced the original question "Who is my neighbor?" into another: "How should I be a good neighbor?" This becomes evident in the question Jesus asked the jurist in the end: "Which of the three proved to be a neighbor to the man who fell among robbers?"

---

8. Rom 5:8.
9. Gal 6:2.
10. Matt 12:36–37.

The jurist got the point but he had trouble acknowledging it because the "good neighbor" was a Samaritan, an enemy, an apostate, a reprobate. I wonder if the third traveler in the story had to be a Samaritan. Evidently Jesus made the good traveler in the story a Samaritan for a reason. The Samaritans had split away from the Israelite community in the ancient past. It was scarcely imaginable to the jurist that a person from that heretical community could do anything worthy of emulation. And here, as Jesus told the story, it was a Samaritan who had shown love to a person in distress. And in contrast the religious figures in the jurist's own tradition had failed to live up to their own rules. Jesus seems to have crafted the story to challenge the jurist's prejudices. In the end the jurist could only acknowledge that the good traveler was "the one who showed mercy."

So what are the religious rules that Jesus, the great teacher, told us to perform? It's simple: go and do likewise.

6

Social Revolution in the Two Letters to Philemon

PEOPLE HAVE NOTED THAT the writers of the New Testament and the early church never condemned the practice of slavery. In Roman times, of course, slavery was taken for granted. Comfortably distant as I am from that abusive system in my own country's past, it is easy for me to be repelled by the whole idea of humans enslaving other humans. Slavery is still practiced in some places today.[1] Repulsive as it is, why didn't the early church condemn it?

In this chapter, I want to examine how the apostle Paul dealt with a problem over a slave that arose in an early Christian community. What Paul did and taught would have a profound impact on the way the slave was treated in that community. And it provides a perspective on how Paul thought about the way Christians should treat each other in a society as stratified as the Romans were, and it also displays a way followers of Christ should regard each other in their respective social statuses.

---

1. "Countries That Still Have Slavery 2025."

Paul was following Jesus in the way he dealt with the situation. And Jesus behaved in a way that cut across the social categories that were recognized in the society of his time. The men he chose as disciples came from different elements of the society, from Simon the Zealot, who presumably had been involved in a movement to drive out the Romans from Palestine, to Matthew, who was employed as a tax collector for the Romans. When he began his role as a rabbi he declared that the kingdom of God had come. And in this kingdom, he said, the poor, the peacemakers, and the meek were blessed by God. In this kingdom people should not "lord over" others but they should serve others.[2] In this kingdom people should "love their neighbors as themselves."[3] They should, in effect, "wash one another's feet."[4] They should show love in the way he had loved them.[5] This was a kingdom sharply different from the kingdoms of the world. To Pilate Jesus said, "My kingdom is not of this world. If it were, my servants would fight to prevent my arrest by the Jewish leaders."[6] The world Jesus stood for was based on a different order of power, organized around different principles, and animated by love.

Paul, who had once persecuted Jesus's followers, had become a dedicated follower of Jesus himself. After he had encountered Christ, he spent at least fourteen years essentially on his own, studying the life and teachings of Jesus, matching them to the prophesies about the Messiah in the Jewish Scriptures.[7] That time of private study and worship of Christ shaped the way Paul would understand the gospel and the special role of service that Christ called him to. Years later, when he came to know a runaway slave who wanted to follow Jesus, that knowledge informed the way Paul would advise him on how to live out his new relationship with Jesus. He should, said Paul, give himself up to his former master.

2. Matt 20:25–28.
3. Matt 19:19; 22:39; Mark 12:31, 33; Luke 10:27; Lev 19:18.
4. John 13.
5. John 15:12; 13:34.
6. John 18:36.
7. Gal 1:18; 2:1.

In this case, Paul seems to show respect for the practice of slavery. But the relationship between master and slave that he proposed for this man, Onesimus, and his master, Philemon, would break radically from the way slavery was practiced in that society. To protect Onesimus Paul wrote a letter to his former master, Philemon, asking him to be generous to Onesimus. Later generations of Christians are fortunate to have the letter Paul addressed to Philemon on behalf of Onesimus, and also another letter, which was addressed to the church in Philemon's house.

The critical moment when Onesimus presented himself at the door of his former master is believed to have taken place in AD 55 (possibly AD 62, depending on which of Paul's imprisonments he refers to in the letter). I want to examine these two letters for what they reveal about Paul's conception of slavery and the way that followers of Jesus should behave toward each other, even if they have different social statuses such as slave and master in a society. I will suggest that Paul's proposal for how these two should relate to each other thereafter constituted a radical break from the customs of the times and undermined the practice of slavery within the Christian community.

THE FIRST LETTER TO PHILEMON

People may dispute whether two letters were sent to Philemon by the apostle Paul, but, if there were two as I suggest, certainly the letter addressed personally to Philemon would have been the first one opened. This was the one that specifically sought to protect the former slave who was at that moment courageously presenting himself at Philemon's door.

The situation would have astonished Philemon. A runaway slave was risking his life by appearing before him unprotected. Such an act was inconceivable in that world. Philemon would have read the note that was presented to him with great interest. Addressed to Philemon, it was signed by Paul, a dear friend. After a warm greeting to Philemon and his family Paul writes to protect Onesimus. "I appeal to you for my son Onesimus, who became my son while I was in chains.... I am sending him—who is my very heart—back to you."[8] Paul said, "I would have liked to keep him with me," but "for love's sake... I did not want to do anything without your consent, so that any favor you do would not seem forced but would be voluntary."[9]

The apostle interposes himself in Onesimus's place. "If you consider me a partner, welcome him as you would welcome me. If he has done you any wrong or owes you anything, charge it to me." And here Paul refers to his own claims over Philemon: "Not to mention that you owe me your very self."[10] To this he further refers to his authority as "an old man and now also a prisoner of Christ Jesus."[11]

Paul seeks more than to save Onesimus's life: he wants him to be restored to Philemon's household. And here Paul plays on Onesimus's name ("useful"): "Formerly he was useless to you, but now he has become useful both to you and to me.... I would have liked to keep him with me so that he could take your place in helping me while I am in chains for the gospel."[12]

And despite all the leverage over Philemon that Paul claims here, he asks Philemon to do this willingly, of his own will. "But I did not want to do anything without your consent, so that any favor you do would not seem forced but would be voluntary."[13]

And here Paul pushes his appeal further. He proposes something that was unthinkable in first-century Rome: "Perhaps the reason he was separated from you for a little while was that you might have him back forever—no longer as a slave, but better than a slave, as a dear brother. He is very dear to me but even dearer to you, both as a fellow man and as a brother in the Lord."[14] Paul calls Onesimus "a brother." A slave should become Philemon's brother?

8. Phlm 10:10, 12.
9. Phlm 10:9, 14.
10. Phlm 10:17–19.
11. Phlm 10:9.
12. Phlm 10:11, 13.
13. Phlm 10:14.
14. Phlm 10:15–16.

As a runaway he could rightfully be scourged, even killed. And Paul was asking that he be received by Philemon as a brother, even "a dear brother." Here is a way of thinking about a slave that would have tested the imagination of any slave holder in the Roman empire. The proposal is revolutionary in its social implications. It dissolves the categorical distinction between master and slave and in its stead establishes a bond of kinship.

But it is revolutionary in a less evident sense: in the manner of Paul's appeal. It was an appeal to Philemon's private sensibility—his conscience. How Philemon received Onesimus would be his own personal, private decision, Paul said. This aggrieved slave owner, who held the rights to dispose of a person who had cost him a lot of money by disappearing, is invited to receive the runaway as "a brother," and of his own accord. His right to decide is crucial to what Paul is urging. "But I did not want to do anything without your consent, so that any favor you do would not seem forced but would be voluntary."[15]

Note the language: "voluntary," not "without your consent." Paul deploys the language of personal appeal. He invites Philemon and his family to receive Onesimus willingly, of their own free will. He hopes they will see Onesimus in a new way, as someone who gives himself to their service voluntarily. The former slave has risked showing himself at their door in hopes they will allow him to become a voluntary servant. And Paul is urging them to receive him as a human being like themselves in a new kind of relationship. Onesimus is the son of Paul, their beloved friend and mentor. All this would have been difficult for Philemon to internalize. How could he not have been bewildered? Paul wanted him to receive Onesimus as someone else than a slave; as a brother. And this brother wants to serve him as a brotherly act, on his own accord.

Note what Paul did not say: he did not appeal to God's will. He offered no negative consequences. He did not say, "God wants you to do this." In this modest letter Paul respects Philemon's legal rights, but he also appeals to Philemon's true inner sensibility. He knows that in this moment, with the former slave standing in

---

15. Phlm 10:14.

front of him, Philemon would be taken aback by the situation. He would have to decide on the spot how to react, how he should behave toward a former slave. All the presuppositions, opinions, and judgments that he had acquired through his life were being challenged in the moment. He had grown up in a Roman world, a world structured into a hierarchy of statuses that were taken as natural. In that world, who accepted and forgave a runaway slave? Paul was appealing to Philemon's inner sense of nobility, breaking with a system of relationships that everyone in Philemon's world took for granted. In fact, to fulfill Paul's wish for him, Philemon was supposed to receive Onesimus willingly, not in pretense. How could he? Without grudging? Without regret? The proposal was that Onesimus would serve him as if he were a close kinsman. He would serve Philemon as a brother in Christ and do it voluntarily, of his own free will.

But for all his gracious and gentle appeal, Paul is still willing to invoke his leverage over Philemon. "Confident of your obedience, I write to you, knowing that you will do even more than I ask. And one thing more: Prepare a guest room for me, because I hope to be restored to you in answer to your prayers."[16] Powerful leverage. Paul wants to come and see how genuinely Philemon fulfilled what Paul was asking.

So there were several devices by which Paul sought to influence Philemon: he asserted his love for Onesimus, he asserted his special relationship to Onesimus, he offered to cover all his material debts to Philemon, he indicated that Onesimus could be "useful" as "a brother," and he intimated that Paul himself would soon come to see how Philemon had carried out his request.

But there is more. The letter is actually addressed to "Philemon our dear friend and fellow worker—also to Apphia our sister and Archippus our fellow soldier—and to the church that meets in your home." Apphia and Archippus, it is reasonable to assume, are relatives of Philemon: Apphia, a woman's name, was presumably his wife and Archippus (a male name) their son. What would Apphia and Archippus say about this proposal? Will they receive

16. Phlm 10:21–22.

Onesimus as a brother? And what about "the church that meets in your home"? Was the whole church supposed to know about this letter? Should it be read to them? This impassioned plea on the behalf of a runaway slave was to be presented to the whole church that met in Philemon's house. It was not merely that Paul wanted Philemon and his family to take Onesimus back, but also for the whole church to take him back, and as a brother.

That the letter to Philemon was preserved suggests how it was received. Philemon would have destroyed it if he had been offended by the letter. Indeed, recognizing the Christian context of this social situation, if Philemon had refused to accept this repentant slave, what could he claim from God? Could Philemon claim the mercy of God if he had refused to forgive Onesimus? Jesus's story of the unmerciful servant surely was known in this community: "'Shouldn't you have had mercy on your fellow servant just as I had on you?' said the master."[17] The very existence of the letter seems to prove that Philemon had not been offended by Paul's appeal—also, that the small community of believers who gathered in his house to worship Christ had also received Onesimus as a brother.

Besides the importance of this letter as a relic of Paul's personal life and ministry it also serves well as an example of Christ's role as an advocate for sinners before the Father. Christ appeals to God for the unworthy: "If he has done you any wrong or owes you anything, charge it to me."[18] The role of Christ before the Father as our advocate is explicated in the letter to the Hebrews. Christ became "merciful and faithful high priest in service to God, . . . that he might make atonement for the sins of the people."[19] Christ has "entered heaven itself, now to appear for us in God's presence."[20] I wonder how quickly Paul's defense of Onesimus before Philemon was compared to the role of Christ before the Father. Once we understand Christ's role as our advocate it is not hard to see how Paul's appeal to Philemon came to be regarded an example of

17. Matt 18:33.
18. Phlm 1:18.
19. Heb 2:17.
20. Heb 9:24.

Christ's appeal to the Father on our behalf. In any case, the similarity was not missed by the church leaders in the fourth century who agreed that it should be included in the list of writings considered authoritative in their community.

The letter was not composed as a challenge to the practice of slavery in Roman society but it reflected a radically different view of human relations. It is, in its implications and assumptions essentially revolutionary. It exposes a social order of a radically different sort than what was normal practice in Roman times—radically different in that it was based on different principles, different assumptions. True, the principles and assumptions of that other social order are not confronted in this letter. But there was another letter, and that one had a lot to say about how that other social order was constituted. And it also was addressed to the church that met in Philemon's house.

THE SECOND LETTER TO PHILEMON

What is implicit in the first letter on the behest of a slave is explicated in the second. The connection between these two letters, therefore, must be established before I can develop this point. We normally call the second letter by another name, the letter of Paul to the church at Colosse. Of course, we don't normally read the letter to the Colossians as a companion to Paul's letter to Philemon, but I want to note here how the perspective that Paul presents in the first letter is explained and amplified in the letter to the Colossians.

Yes, the two letters are connected. The evidences for this connection are the references to individuals in the letters. Figures 1, 2, and 3 match the names mentioned in the two letters: those with Paul, some of whom have given Paul information on the Colossian church (figure 1); those in the target community (figure 2); and those arriving with the two letters (figure 3). The same people are with Paul in both letters. Those mentioned with him in the letter to the Colossian church are Epaphras, Aristarchus, Mark, Jesus called Justice, Luke, and Demas. Those mentioned in Philemon are the same except that there is no mention of "Jesus called Justice." Also, in both letters Archippus is mentioned, and in each case he appears to have a similar role: in Philemon he is called "our fellow soldier," presumably in serving the church; in Colossians he is given a directive that fits that role: "See to it that you complete the ministry you have received in the Lord."[21] Also, Onesimus is mentioned in Colossians and there Paul makes a point of commending him: "Onesimus, our faithful and dear brother, who is one of you."[22] Tychicus is mentioned in Colossians but not in Philemon; he would have been the bearer the letter to the Colosse church and if the two letters are, as I am suggesting, connected, he was the bearer of the letter to Philemon. Out of the twelve names mentioned in these two notes, ten of them overlap. And each person mentioned is in the same place and in the same condition (in or out of prison).

Figure 1. Individuals with Paul

Letter to Colosse	People Mentioned with Paul	Letter to Philemon
Col 4:18	Paul, a prisoner	V. 1
Col 1:7–8: You learned it from Epaphras, our dear fellow servant, . . . and who also told us of your love in the Spirit. 4:12–13: Epaphras, who is one of you. . . . He is always wrestling in prayer for you, . . . working hard for you.	Epaphras	V. 23: My fellow prisoner in Christ Jesus
Col 4:10	Aristarchus	V. 24
Col 4:10	Mark	V. 24
Col 4:11	Jesus = Justice	(unmentioned)
Col 4:14	Luke	V. 24
Col 4:14	Demas	V. 24

---

21. Col 4:17.
22. Col 4:9.

Figure 2. Individuals in the Target Community

Letter to Colosse	People in the Target Community	Letter to Philemon
Unmentioned	Philemon	V. 1: To Philemon
Unmentioned	Apphia	V. 1: Our sister
Col 4:17: Tell Archippus: See to it that you complete the work you have received in the Lord.	Archippus	V. 2: Our fellow soldier

Figure 3. Individuals Arriving with the Letters

Letter to Colosse	People Arriving	Letter to Philemon
Col 4:9: Our faithful and dear brother who is one of you.	Onesimus	Vv. 10ff, (arriving with the letter)
Col 4:7: [He is] coming with Onesimus.	Tychicus	(An unnamed bearer of the letter)

In Colossians some the individuals with Paul—Aristarchus, Epaphras, Mark, Luke, and Demas—may have been in prison with him, although only the first two are so mentioned. In Philemon the only one in prison mentioned with Paul was Epaphras.

It looks like the church that met in Philemon's house was the church that Paul wrote his letter to. The letters came as a pair. I'd like here to look in the letter to the Colossians for what it reveals about the problem addressed in the note to Philemon. While the first letter was written to protect Onesimus, the second, addressed to the church that meets in Philemon's house, was written that the community that met in Colosse understood how the gospel of Christ bore on many parts of their lives. Included among the implications that Paul mentions were how slaves should behave toward their masters and masters to their slaves.

Slaves are mentioned in two places in Colossians. The first is buried in a paragraph concerned with more general things. Paul has already set forth Christ as supreme over all things, and here he is explaining how Christ's authority and saving work bears on how his followers should act out their faith in the world. Christ's work should influence the way they approach their ordinary affairs. "Since, then, you have been raised with Christ, set your hearts on things above, where Christ is, seated at the right hand of God. Set your minds on things above, not on earthly things. For you died, and your life is now hidden with Christ in God."[23] Accordingly, they are to "put to death, therefore, whatever belongs to your earthly nature: sexual immorality, impurity, lust, evil desires and greed, which is idolatry." Also, they are to abandon "anger, rage, malice, slander, and filthy language" as well as deceit. And besides "putting to death" such practices they should ignore the social distinctions that are extant in their worldly setting. "Here there is no gentile or Jew, circumcised or uncircumcised, barbarian, Scythian, slave or free, but Christ is all, and is in all."[24] This special attention to "slave" with no comparable reference to "master" could not have been missed by either Philemon or Onesimus. As believers should set aside the practices of the past such as fornication and the like, they should similarly ignore their respective statuses in the wider society. Social distinctions are dissolved in a community in which "Christ is all and in all."

They are to put to death "whatever belongs to your earthly nature," and they are to clothe themselves with "the new nature," treating each other with "compassion, kindness, humility, gentleness and patience." And to this list Paul adds this: "Bear with each other and forgive one another if any of you has a grievance against someone. Forgive as the Lord forgave you." Could the folks in this congregation have missed the pointed reference to the concerns of Philemon and Onesimus? I don't think so. Paul adds to the above,

---

23. Col 3:1–3.

24. Col 3:10–11. The word "Scythian" stands out as different in kind from the other terms used in this sentence. Scythians were central Asian marauding bands that had for generations harassed the settled populations that were settled near the steppe lands of central Asia. This included Anatolia where Colosse was located. Why were Scythians mentioned here? Could Onesimus have been a captive from a clash with the Scythians?

"And over all these virtues put on love, which binds them all together in perfect unity."[25]

To explain what this means for the folks in this community Paul takes up the problem of relationships between some of the categorical distinctions that they have to live with in practice; wives and husbands, children and parents, slaves and masters. In this second reference to slaves Paul has more to say for slaves than masters. Its relevance to Onesimus could not have been missed by him and everyone else in the church: "Slaves, obey your earthly masters in everything; and do it, not only when their eye is on you and to curry their favor, but with sincerity of heart and reverence for the Lord. Whatever you do, work at it with all your heart, as working for the Lord, not for human masters, since you know that you will receive an inheritance from the Lord as a reward. It is the Lord Christ you are serving."[26] Three times Paul indicates that slaves are to work for their masters as if they were serving the Lord. As for the masters, Paul has less to say. "Masters, provide your slaves with what is right and fair, because you know that you also have a Master in heaven."[27] Both slave and master are to live oriented toward their heavenly master, Christ, who bought his rights over them by his death and resurrection.

FINAL OBSERVATIONS

Note how large are the implications of the death and resurrection of Jesus for this community. For them, including Philemon and Onesimus, it meant a new way of life, a new way to behave with each other, a new hope for the future, a new ground of love, a new bond of loyalty and responsibility. It meant a new way to think about events and situations as they arose in their lives. It was a new and different social order, oriented toward a different kind of reality. This was a revolutionary difference, but it was not rebellious. It

---

25. Col 3:12–14.
26. Col 3:22–24.
27. Col 4:1.

did not contest the social statuses of the worldly society of the time. Instead, it was, says Paul, a way of life through whom, animated by God's spiritual help, they would demonstrate the character of their savior in the society of their time. They were to live out what their master in heaven was like.

All this is developed in the second letter sent to Philemon by Paul. It constructs the frame of reference within which, for the Christian, all of life is to be lived. As Christ willingly gave himself up to his enemies, died an ignoble death and rose from that death, he became the source of an eternal salvation for everyone who willingly embraces his mercy out of grateful hearts. It should be evinced in the way they live out their gratitude by obeying the directives of Christ such as those presented by Paul in his letters to Philemon and the church in Colosse.

And, by the way, do we know what happened to Onesimus? The letters themselves provide no information on how they were received. But there are clues: one, of course, is the fact that the two letters survived. The very existence of Paul's letter to Philemon implies that Philemon, his family, and his church accepted Onesimus into their employ, as Paul had urged. But there is one helpful clue. The early church father Ignatius indicates that someone named Onesimus became much admired in the early church community. In a letter to the church at Ephesus, he says that Onesimus is "a man of inexpressible love, and your bishop in the flesh, whom I pray you by Jesus Christ to love, and that you would all seek to be like him. And blessed be he who has granted unto you, being worthy, to obtain such an excellent bishop."[28] The high praise for this Onesimus suggests that he became a beloved leader in the

---

28. See Ignatius, *Epistles of Ignatius*, loc. 10. According to the Wikipedia entry on Onesimus, "It may be the case that this Onesimus was the same one consecrated a bishop by the apostles, and who accepted the episcopal throne in Ephesus following Timothy. Whether in the reign of Roman emperor Domitian or the persecution of Trajan, Onesimus was imprisoned in Rome. He may have been martyred by stoning (some sources claim he was beheaded). However, since the reign of Domitian was from AD 81 to 96, and that of Trajan lasted to AD 117, Onesimus's death would have to fall within these years." See "Onesimus," under § In Tradition.

Christian movement. If this is the runaway slave Paul wrote his letter for, it seems clear that his estimation of him as a "faithful and beloved brother" was proven in the service he gave to the church.[29]

Besides Ignatius's reference to Onesimus there is another ancient reference to someone named Onesimus. The Eastern Orthodox church recognizes Onesimus as "the Bishop of Byzantium."[30]

---

29. Col 4:9.

30. The Greek Orthodox Church honors him as a saint. See "Apostle Onesimus."

7

Political Uses of Religious Zeal

IN THE PASSAGE BELOW, the zeal of some Jews for their sacred tradition, the Ten Commandments, displayed the difference between espousing the commandments and actually living by the standards of the commandments.

> Now Stephen, a man full of God's grace and power, performed great wonders and signs among the people. Opposition arose, however, from members of the Synagogue of the Freedmen (as it was called)—Jews of Cyrene and Alexandria as well as the provinces of Cilicia and Asia—who began to argue with Stephen. But they could not stand up against the wisdom the Spirit gave him as he spoke. Then they secretly persuaded some men to say, "We have heard Stephen speak blasphemous words against Moses and against God." So they stirred up the people and the elders and the teachers of the law. They seized Stephen and brought him before the Sanhedrin. They produced false witnesses, who testified, "This fellow never stops speaking against this holy place and against the law. For we have heard him say that this Jesus

of Nazareth will destroy this place and change the customs Moses handed down to us."[1]

The name "Synagogue of the Freedmen" suggests that this synagogue had been founded by former slaves.[2] But it leaves unclear whether the "freedmen" worshipped by themselves or with Jews from the regions named in the text. The term implies that the synagogue could have been founded by former slaves who had settled in Jerusalem. Is this the founders' generation or a later generation? We have no clue. What the author makes clear is that these were Jews from abroad or descendants of Jews from abroad; he specifically cites the places they are from: North Africa (Cyrene and Alexandria) and Asia Minor (Cilicia and Asia). One wonders how aliens from such distant and disparate places got together. Could this have been the synagogue for foreigners?

That they were in some sense marginal Jews seems important for the story, as the author takes pains to identify the name of the synagogue (Synagogue of the Freedmen) and the foreign places its members were from. This was not a usual group of Jews.[3]

Can we then surmise that their marginality was a factor in their behavior? As former slaves, or at least as alien Jews transplanted from elsewhere into the heart of the Jewish sacred community, they would have thought it important to demonstrate their bona fides as "real" Jews. In the affair described here, are these Jews trying to win acceptance? Trying to be "more Jewish" than the natives of Jerusalem? Whatever their motive, they seem to be the only (or at least the main) Jews in Jerusalem who engaged with Stephen over his Christian faith.

Also, if Stephen was a Samaritan, as has been proposed,[4] then it is possible that the members of this synagogue felt they could press their case against him because he was more marginal than they, not only because he was a Samaritan (if he was), but also

1. Acts 6:8–14.

2. The various commentaries on this passage have little certainty on what this synagogue was. See "Synagogue of the Libertines."

3. Douglas, *New Bible Dictionary*, 386.

4. Munck, *Acts of the Apostles*, 285–300.

because of course he was an outspoken voice for a new movement that had been publicly opposed by the chief priests. Something about this group, this synagogue, was different, distinct from the rest in that they—unlike other Jews—instigated and pressed the charges against Stephen. Their instigation of this affair reveals a zeal, as they put it, for "the Holy Place" and "the law."

But, it turns out, they were willing to break the regulations of the law in order to promote it. They produced "false witnesses" to testify against Stephen. This was contrary to the ninth commandment, "You shall not bear false witness against your neighbor." So, in this situation it was not the careful observance of the law that mattered for them so much as their intent to display their allegiance to the law. In such a case the law becomes a symbol of their religious piety, their zeal for Jewish solidarity. The law was for them in this case a useful political device. The thoughtful, reflective practice of the ten rules of life was not the point here. It was instead a chance to parade their passion for the Jewish tradition. The law was deployed to flourish their religious zeal as sincere Jews. They claimed that Stephen was speaking against "the Holy Place" and "the law" (v. 13), terms that are glossed in the next verse as "this place" and "the customs Moses handed down to us." The term "law" in v. 13 becomes "customs" in v. 14. So another nuance of their claim against Stephen was its implication that Jewish custom was at stake. The Mosaic law here stands for customary virtues. Holy place, law, Moses, customary practice—these terms are flaunted over-eagerly. The Jews of the Freedmen's synagogue were sucking up to the leading figures in their community by bringing Stephen before the Sanhedrin.

The Ten Commandments work well as an emblem of public virtues, but the honest truth is that some of them are actually difficult to practice: "You shall not covet your neighbor's wife. You shall not set your desire on your neighbor's house or land . . . or anything that belongs to your neighbor."[5] The public flaunting of the Commandments is easy to do. Putting them into practice, living by such rules is something different altogether.

5. Deut 5:21.

POLITICAL USES OF RELIGIOUS ZEAL

Once anything becomes deployed for political purposes—however good it may be in itself—it becomes a device to deceive or misrepresent. In politics, hypocrisy pervades. This appears to be what animated the zeal of the Jews from the Freedmen Synagogue, a zeal that would cost Stephen's life.

8

Peter's Little-Noted Statement About Peoples "From Every Nation"

God does not show favoritism but accepts from every nation the one who fears him and does what is right.[1]

MUCH HAS BEEN MADE of Peter's great declaration, "You are the Christ, the Son of the Living God!"[2] and deservedly so. But Peter put into words two other insights of importance, whose significance, it seems to me, has been little remarked by many in the Christian community. These other statements appear in Luke's narrative of the early history of the church, in Acts 10. Events described in that passage marked a dramatic turn in the history of the church, and it was Peter who formulated a spiritual insight that he and his Jewish Christian colleagues had not seen before. As Peter put his new thoughts into words, each at a strategic moment, each in a

1. Acts 10:34b–35.
2. Matt 16:16.

particularly clear and decisive language, he formulated a new perspective on the world and his place in it. Possibly, what came out of his mouth surprised even him as much as the other Jews who were with him. And yet it was authentically Peter's own thought, his own logical construction from what he had experienced.

He came to see what he saw, and to understand what he understood, experientially, just as he had experienced Jesus. One wonders if it could have happened any other way, for it was a remarkable turn of mind. He would, in effect, state that contrary to custom a Jew could not only agree to have fellowship with a gentile in the worship of God, but also invite him into his house, have dinner with him, and enter his home—and, even more surprising, that the God of heaven would grant the same spiritual status to a gentile as to a Jew. Here is the story of how he came to such a radical turn of mind.

THE CONTEXT

This was a time when the Christian community had begun to be dispersed, owing to persecution: "They were all scattered throughout the region of Judea and Samaria, except the apostles."[3] But the persecution seemed to abate and the gospel was prospering: Paul's conversion had recently taken place (chapter 9); the church had been advancing well "throughout Judea, Galilee and Samaria";[4] and Peter had healed a paralytic and even raised a woman from the dead.[5]

The focus shifts to the city of Caesarea where a centurion had a remarkable experience. In the meantime, Peter was in Joppa where he had raised the woman from the dead. This is a Roman city, probably not inhabited by many Jews.

The Jews and Romans normally kept apart. The Romans probably had little interest in Jewish affairs (as appears in several parts

---

3. Acts 8:1.
4. Acts 9:31.
5. Acts 9:32–42.

of Acts); the Jews regarded the Romans as unclean and so avoided much contact with them (as our story reveals in chapter 10).

THE CHARACTERS

Cornelius was a centurion in the Italian Regiment. Luke says he was "a devout man who feared God with all his household, gave alms liberally to the people, and prayed constantly to God."[6] His servants said of him, "He is a righteous and God-fearing man, who is respected by all the Jewish people."[7] This was the kind of man who even though he was a commander of one hundred Roman legionnaires, when confronted with a man of God (Peter), he fell down before him—unusual behavior for a Roman officer before a Jew.[8]

This man "distinctly saw an angel of God," who told him that "your prayers and gifts to the poor have come up as a memorial offering before God." And the angel directed him to send for Peter for a special message. And he gave him Peter's whereabouts in detail: "He is lodging with Simon, a tanner, whose house is by the seaside."[9]

Peter's special importance in the extension of the gospel was implied by Jesus when he said he would give to him "the keys to the kingdom."[10] Whatever that meant Peter not only sometimes captured in his own words the beliefs and opinions of the other disciples—"You are the Messiah of God"—but also here, in this encounter with the centurion, formulated some concepts important to the story that Luke was telling in the book of Acts. These statements came out of him spontaneously but captured a perception that was necessary for the early church to embrace as the gospel expanded to the gentiles. His experience, described here, was significant for him personally, but more importantly, the observations that he made of

---

6. Acts 10:1–2.
7. Acts 10:22.
8. Acts 10:25.
9. Acts 10:4–6.
10. Matt 16:19.

the situation before him became significant for the wider community of Christians, because it revealed something about the gospel that they had not yet realized: that God was working among the Gentiles as well as the Jews and the news that Christ had come had a comparable relevance to them as well as to the Jews.

THE CHALLENGE TO PETER'S IMAGINATION

Peter's experience began in Joppa. It was "on the following day"—that is, after Cornelius had his vision and before Peter heard about it. On that day he had a dream in which three times he was confronted with animals that Jews would not eat. Three times he told to eat of those creatures, and when he recoiled, a voice responded, "Do not call anything impure that God has made clean."[11] Peter was pondering what this could mean when Cornelius's men from Caesarea—gentiles—found him.

Again the Spirit spoke to him, this time to tell him to go down to meet the men and to go with them. Peter, a Jew, invited these men, gentiles, into the house. He was a guest in that house but he nevertheless invited them into this Jewish house. The text gives no clue as how others in that house reacted. In any case, that invitation was an astonishing act. Evidently, the others in that house did not object to Peter's decision to bring these gentile strangers into their house, no doubt in deference to Peter. Here was a new experience for Peter and those with him.

The next day he and some the "brothers," Christianized Jews no doubt, set out with the gentiles on the journey to meet Cornelius. It was thirty miles to Caesarea and the journey would have taken a full day, assuming they were traveling on horseback. When Peter finally arrived, Cornelius fell at his feet in reverence. Peter refused to allow it and declared himself to be "only a man myself." Cornelius in any case grasped the spiritual significance of the occasion, for he said to Peter, "We are all here present in the sight of God, to hear all that you have been commanded by the Lord to tell us."[12]

11. Acts 10:15.
12. Acts 10:33.

It is curious that Luke says that "as he talked," Peter entered a room filled with people. They were no doubt all gentiles, Cornelius's friends as well as members of his family. Cornelius, we have noted, was an upright man, but he was not alone in being upright: many others were there also, eager to hear what Peter would tell them.

TWO ENTIRELY NOVEL FORMULATIONS

Peter will tell the story of Jesus and in the process he makes two statements of great importance to Luke's narrative and, as it would happen, to the church in this nascent period of the advance of the gospel. The first of these was this:

> You are well aware that it is against our law for a Jew to associate with or visit a Gentile. But God has shown me that I should not call anyone impure or unclean.[13]

He was referring of course to the vision he had had on the previous day, which had so mystified him. But now it began to make sense when his guides arrived with the invitation from Cornelius, an event no one could have anticipated. On the way he and his fellow travelers, Jews and gentiles together, had had several hours to talk about spiritual matters. How could Peter not have described to his guides the coming of Jesus, the betrayal and death of Jesus, his resurrection, his appearances to Peter afterward, the exciting day of Pentecost when the Holy Spirit fell upon the community of believers in Jerusalem, the rapid expansion of the gospel message to neighboring communities. And now there was this surprising turn of events, Peter's vision and the special request from Cornelius—all this was working on Peter's conception of what God was doing.

Peter, and possibly also his Jewish companions, had grasped what the vision meant: a Jew could call no one impure; human beings are all the same, on the same standing with God. What a radical idea for a Jew! The vision and the events as they would transpire would open up, for Peter and his Jewish companions, a

---

13. Acts 10:28.

world of new possibilities, a new vision, a far grander conception of God's project to reach the world with the good news.

By the time they had reached Caesarea, Peter was able to put into words the profound revolutionary implications of what he was learning about the gospel that he had been preaching, that the gentiles and Jews were indistinguishable in the eyes of God: "God has shown me that I should not call any man common or unclean." He had no grounds for separating himself from gentiles, for he and they were spiritually on the same plane in the eyes of God. The point was so significant to him that Peter says it again in the opening lines of his second letter to the dispersed Christians of Asia Minor: "To those who through the righteousness of our God and Savior Jesus Christ have received a faith as precious as ours."[14] Jews and gentiles have equal standing before God: a radical idea for a Jew.

Cornelius immediately told Peter about his encounter with the angel and then said, "It was good of you to come," recognizing how significant it was for Peter, a Jew, to come into his house. Then he urged his visitor to speak: "We are all here present in the sight of God, to hear all that you have been commanded by the Lord."[15] Cornelius, and presumably his guests, recognized that this was a momentous situation. They were, as he said, "in the presence of God."

Peter's response in this setting was conceptually as momentous as the first statement, if not more so—at least for anyone who was a Jew. The concept he then put into words, again a formulation expressed for the first time, captured a significant insight for the Christian church, which until then had thought of the gospel movement as essentially a Jewish movement. Peter of course recognized that Cornelius was an upright man. This was eminently manifest in many details that had just been revealed to Peter:

- Cornelius's worship of God
- His gifts to the poor

14. 2 Pet 1:1.
15. Acts 10:33.

- His courteous treatment of the Jewish subject people
- The authorization that he had received by the appearance of an angel
- What the angel declared to him: that his prayers and alms had ascended to heaven as a memorial offering
- The explicit direction to find a man named Peter in Joppa, who would give him a special message

All this brought Peter to put into words an amazing statement, "I now realize how true it is that God does not show favoritism but accepts from every nation the one who fears him and does what is right."[16] Here it is, stated by a Jew. The notion that God accepts people from every nation who fear him and do what is right—this is a formulation so comprehensive, so expansive, that it can barely be grasped. Luke has traced the stages of Peter's education from life as a fisherman to an apostle of a gospel for the world. First, was his call by Jesus, then his confession "You are the Messiah," then his denial and remorse and eventual his restitution, then his role in speaking out for the Christian community on the day of Pentecost, declaring that no other name existed under heaven by which we may be saved. And here there is yet another stage in his growth in understanding of the gospel. Peter's encounter with Cornelius would mark a milestone in understanding and vision that Peter and his Jewish Christian colleagues would come to embrace. This concept—that God accepts people from every nation who fear him and do what is right—was contrary to all that they had learned as Jews. It was a revolution in thought.

Peter makes this statement in the presence of his Jewish colleagues. He was the one who put this concept into words, but it was surely an issue about which he and his fellow travelers to Caesarea, Jews and gentiles together, would have already talked about. Between Peter's vision in Joppa and their arrival to the house of Cornelius in Caesarea, not only Peter but those with him had pondered the significance of the vision and their invitation from Cornelius. And they were about to see how timely it was, for this

16. Acts 10:34–35.

encounter with Cornelius would open up horizons beyond what any of them could ever have imagined.

Luke does not present this as a creative insight out of nothing: it came as the apostle and his friends reflected on the vision and matched it with the specific developments they experienced in this affair. The insight was a conclusion naturally constructed from personal experience, through events that were both private (Peter's vision) and public (the visit by gentile messengers from Cornelius).

The progression of understanding continued as Peter and his Jewish friends came to understand that gentiles exist who fear God, whom God receives as he had received them and other believing Jews. And it would be an insight authorized by a dramatic event. Peter tells the story of Jesus to these gentiles including the commission given him. He concludes with this assertion: "And he commanded us to preach to the people, and to testify that he is the one ordained by God to be judge of the living and the dead. To him all the prophets bear witness that everyone who believes in him receives forgiveness of sins through his name."[17] At that moment, "while Peter was still speaking these words, the Holy Spirit came on all who heard the message."[18]

We wonder what that was. What actually happened? What did Peter see? Whatever that "coming upon" of the Spirit was, it was visible, objective, irrefutably real. And its spiritual power was unmistakable. Peter would stress that point when he had to defend himself before his Jewish Christian friends in Jerusalem. "As I began to speak, the Holy Spirit came on them as he had come on us at the beginning. Then I remembered what the Lord had said: 'John baptized with water, but you will be baptized with the Holy Spirit.' So if God gave them the same gift he gave us who believed in the Lord Jesus Christ, who was I to think that I could stand in God's way?"[19]

---

17. Acts 10:42–43.
18. Acts 10:44.
19. Acts 11:15–17.

Whatever the display of the Holy Spirit's power among the gentiles was, it demonstrated to Peter and his Jewish colleagues that gentiles were being grafted into the nascent church, received into the church on an equal plane with the Jewish Christians. The gentiles—folks who had little or no knowledge of the Jewish tradition or of God's ways—were shown in that moment to be accepted by the Holy Spirit into the believing community. They would soon take key roles in the advance of the gospel; they provided a new creative impulse in the proclamation of the good news to the wider world.

It would eventually reach an ignorant gentile like me. Admittedly unworthy of his mercy, I am now fully accepted into the community of God's family, a standing as good as all the rest, even the apostles.[20]

> Oh, the depth of the riches of the wisdom and knowledge of God! How unsearchable his judgments, and his paths beyond tracing out! "Who has known the mind of the Lord? Or who has been his counselor?" "Who has ever given to God, that God should repay them?" For from him and through him and for him are all things. To him be the glory forever! Amen."[21]

---

20. 2 Pet 1:2.

21. Rom 11:33–36.

9

"My God! You Are a Mussulman Man Like Me!"

THIS CHAPTER IS ABOUT a conversation between me, an anthropologist, and a peasant farmer who lived in a relatively isolated village in central Afghanistan.[1] In this conversation, some of the presuppositions of the farmer about foreigners (*khārejis*) like me were overturned by some of the things he learned about me, my faith, and the world that I came from. In the end, he spontaneously pronounced me a moral person like himself. I conclude with a discussion of how our interpersonal conversations can lead to deeper personal relationships.

It is not uncommon for people in one religious tradition to suppose that folks in other religions are less pious, less moral than themselves, maybe even condemned to hell as unbelievers.[2] This chapter is about the mutual surprise of two strangers to discover

---

1. This is a revision and extension on an article by the same title in *On Knowing Humanity* 9:1 (2025) (CC BY 4.0).
2. Accad and Andrews, *Religious Other*.

that, despite their contrary religious backgrounds, they could recognize in the other a common ground of humanity.

The conversation was between me and a peasant farmer named Khodāhdād,[3] whom I met in 1967 in an isolated valley high in the Hindu Kush Mountains of Afghanistan. I had gone to Afghanistan to study the diverse customs of the people of the country and like others doing field work I brought to the project my own moral presumptions—presumptions that would be tested, as often happens to us when we come to know people unlike ourselves. As my conversation with Khodāhdād entailed a confrontation of different religious presumptions, it seems imperative that I reveal some details of the moral perspective that I brought to that moment.

MY BACKGROUND

I grew up in Tulsa, Oklahoma, and as a high school student I became involved in a Christian movement known as Young Life. When I went to university I became active in a similar organization, InterVarsity Christian Fellowship. Through the people I came to know and admire in those organizations I made a serious personal commitment to follow Christ as I best knew how. As it happened, however, throughout my university experience I was struggling with a problem I had with God, for he was not answering my prayers about an issue that was deeply painful to me. Eventually, I decided to seek a more specific understanding of the faith that I had espoused. While I knew a number of proof texts in the Bible, I knew little about the Bible as a whole, so I set out to read it in hopes I could better understand what I had gotten into. That decision would be the most significant educational experience of my life as an undergraduate student. By the time I graduated I had read thoughtfully through the whole Bible almost twice, and I came away from the experience with a different perspective on myself, my sense of what God was like, and what he was doing in human affairs. Honestly, I don't think the problem that had spurred my reading project had been resolved. But

---

3. The name is fictitious.

now it seemed less compelling, and it was by then absorbed within the grander, more comprehensive view I now had of what the Bible was all about. Of course, there would be much more to learn, and I continued to read regularly through the Bible at my own pace. (It would be some years before I worked out my understanding of how God works among peoples in other societies.) The effect was to generate in me an inner sense of gratitude and I wanted to give myself to a social activity that would seem an appropriate response.

Immediately after graduation I found an opportunity to teach English in Afghanistan. I was happy to sign a contract at the embassy of Afghanistan in Washington, DC when Dr. Tabibi, the Afghan ambassador, asked me not to proselytize my faith in his Muslim country. I agreed. While I was animated to go to Afghanistan because of my faith I did not suppose that what I would be doing would be proselytizing. Anyway, I didn't know how to proselytize in my own language, much less in one I didn't know.

In Kabul, I taught English to Afghan students in the fifth, sixth, seventh, and eighth grades in an old building known as Habibia College, a school instituted in 1903 by King Habibullah Khan. It was a great experience for a twenty-two-year-old that had scarcely ever been outside of Oklahoma. I spent much of my free time trying to learn the local language, Kabuli Persian, now called Dari. I got a tutor and also I sat outside trying to talk to the children playing in my street. It was great fun. But after two years my draft board disallowed me from staying. So I returned to the States where I ended up going to graduate school.

I was able to get back into Afghanistan in 1957 after doing my military service, this time with my new bride, and in the next few years Rita and I produced three children in Kabul. That was our home. This time I was again teaching English as a second language but employed by Teachers College Columbia University, which, as part of the United State Foreign Aid Program, had contracted to work with the Afghan government to develop its education program. Again, an American supervisor from the college, with some embarrassment, asked me to refrain from proselytizing (admitting that what he was doing was "noneducational"). My job was to teach English in the higher grades; I also worked in the production of English language textbooks to be used throughout the country. We stayed in Kabul until late in 1964 when I was admitted into the doctoral program in anthropology at the University of Michigan.

When I returned to Afghanistan in 1966 to undertake anthropological field work, I had studied anthropology and Middle Eastern culture at the University of Michigan and the London University School of Oriental Studies and I still held to my Christian faith. Importantly, I had more facility in speaking Dari. It was exciting to be on the ground and able to undertake serious research among the peoples I had come to enjoy and admire.

THE BAMYAN VALLEY

The location for my field project was the Bamyan Valley, a place famous for the giant Buddhas built by a community that had flourished between the second and eighth centuries. Throughout history, this valley had been a major depot of the central Asian caravan traffic between India and China. The opportunity to do research among the citizens of this famous valley had come to me through the invitation of someone I met in Kabul. He was a local leader in a village in eastern Bamyan near the Shibar Pass. Shibar was the entrée into Bamyan for travelers coming from Kabul. The trip entailed passing through Koh Daman to the Ghorband Valley which eventually reached the base of the pass. Here the road began to rise abruptly as much as two thousand feet through a series of switchbacks to reach the summit of the pass, which is 9,800 feet above sea level. From there the road descends into Bamyan, a narrow east-west plain about forty-five miles long before it begins to rise into the highlands of Qarghanatu. At the center of the valley, where the largest Buddha looms over a small market town, the plain is little more than a mile wide. Above this famous valley ascends the mountains of the Hindu Kush, at its highest point 13,100 feet above sea level.

The eastern boundary of this valley is an escarpment created by the subduction of the South Asian tectonic plate under the

"My God! You Are a Mussulman Man Like Me!"

Eurasian tectonic plate. Shibar is the point where the land is forced upward so that waters flow off it in three directions. From its eastern slopes water descends into the Ghorband Valley to form a river that joins the Kabul River which in turn flows into the Indus which debouches into the Indian Ocean. On the west side of the Shibar escarpment water flows into the Bamyan Valley. At a low point in the valley, the water coming off of Shibar converges with waters coming from Qarghanatu and together they veer northward surging through the narrow Shikari Gorge into the catchment area of the Oxus River. The Oxus once drained into the Aural Sea, but since Soviet times it has been diverted onto the cotton farms of Uzbekistan, leaving the sea slowly to die in the Karakum Desert. Besides the waters flowing east and west off the Shibar escarpment, to the south the land breaks to allow water to flow southward to form the Helmand River. This great river passes near Kandahar and extends into the Registan Desert and dies in salt marshes of the Dasht-e Margo ("Desert of Death") shared with Iran.

The tribal peoples occupying the lands west of Shibar in the Hindu Kush are known as Hazaras, although at the market town below the largest Buddha some people call themselves Tajiks. Most Hazaras identify as Imāmi Shia, ('Ithnā 'Ašaris, "Twelvers") although in Shibar a sizeable community of Ismailis live among them. The East Asian features of these people suggest that the Hazaras originated somewhere in the Far East, possibly Mongolia.

In my first year of fieldwork in Bamyan I made biweekly forays into Shibar visiting friends of my patron in several villages. During the second year, I studied the market town at the center of Bamyan. The conversation I describe here took place in spring 1967 in a village of Shibar. I suppose that other than their leaders few folks from this area traveled much beyond the market town.

Of course, in my manner and accent I stood out as a foreigner, a *khārejī*. And by implication I probably was not a Muslim. That is, I was an unbeliever, an infidel, a *kāfir*. This is a Qur'anic term and it meant, as in Surah 26:19, or 16:55, or 30:33, someone who "conceals" something, such as the truth. The term was applied to the Meccans who opposed the prophet early on and so it had the sense of unbelievers, thus an "infidel."[4] The Fiqh scholars trying to organize the obligations of believers used the term to mean someone who was condemned, bound for hell. That *kāfirs* are eternally damned is presumed by most folks in Afghanistan, according to several friends. And with that notion it has come to imply someone who has no scruples, is unclean and sexually promiscuous. A *kāfir*, I was told, will sleep with his mother and his sister. Jeffery Goldberg says of the students in the Daral Uloom madrasa that they believe Americans will "engage in sex with anything anywhere, all the time." When visiting the seminary, Goldberg was asked "whether American men were allowed by law to keep boyfriends and girlfriends at the same time."[5]

In the Hazarajat, the term *kāfir* is connected with certain features of the environment, for the famous Buddha statues and the meditational caves carved into the limestone cliffs evoke a time when these valleys pulsed with a Buddhist civilization in which the people worshipped the giant idols that loom over the valley. This was a center of trade and interaction with the far-flung civilizations of Eurasia. Besides the Buddhas and the caves for meditation that that civilization left behind there were the ruins of their villages built high up in the tributary valleys of Bamyan. These ruins are known locally as *kāfir qalāhs*, "infidel forts." Three times during the two years I was in the highlands of Bamyan someone said to me, in effect, "Your ancestors, your people, built these forts." It was a mystifying statement to me at first, but eventually I came to realize that this was how I fit into their world. I was a *kāfir*, an unbeliever like those who had built those towns, and so they supposed that it had been my people who built those *kāfir qalāhs*. Their own ancestor could not have built them, they reasoned, for their people, as they saw it, had always been Muslims and recoiled from idolatry. To people of Shibar it made sense that my ancestors, *kāfirs* like me, had constructed the *kāfir qalāhs*.

---

4. Surah 1:2.
5 Goldberg, "Inside Jihad U.," para. 56.

"My God! You Are a Mussulman Man Like Me!"

MY INTERLOCUTOR

Khodāhdād was a nonliterate peasant farmer of these highlands, as this account will reveal, little informed about the world I came from. I suspect he had scarcely ever been out of Shibar. So, I avoid calling him a "typical Afghan." Truly, I don't know how to identify such a type anyway, and I am sure that my urban, educated, multilingual Afghan friends in Kabul would have been embarrassed to have Khodāhdād held up as "typical Afghan" of any sort. They would say, as he would say himself, that he was *kohband*, "mountain bound," limited in his local experience to his home in the highlands of Shibar. His place was about three hours on foot to the main road and (in those days) about twelve hours by car to Kabul. I doubt if he had ever been there.

So, it is worth emphasizing that such a conversation could not these days take place anywhere among the Afghanistan peoples. This is not the same world. No Afghan could be unaware of the foreign powers that have been involved in this country through four decades war. The Afghan War of 1978–1992 was started by the Soviet invasion, and the opposition was enabled by money and materiel from the United States and Pakistan, not to mention several other countries of the industrial world. The little remarked internecine war among the Hazaras (1982–1984), in which Hazaras fought bitterly against each other, was largely due to the meddling of Iran. The vicious battle for Kabul in 1992–1996 between several mujahedin organizations was funded by several foreign powers: Iran, Saudi Arabia, and Pakistan. The Taliban's struggle with the Northern Alliance (1996–2001) was supported by Pakistan and Saudi Arabia while their opponents were backed by Iran, India, and Russia. And finally, the Americans' attempt to crush the Taliban (abandoned by the Pakistanis and Saudis) in 2001–2002 was animated by their furious desire to find Osama Bin Laden. Thus, no Afghan, even a farmer in Shibar, could be unaware of the wider world in the current millennium, which is not to say that the people have had reason to abandon their beliefs about foreign *kāfirs*.

THE CONVERSATION

This account of my conversation with Khodāhdād is based on notes taken down immediately after the conversation.

He squatted on the edge of a well-worn cotton rug that his uncle had graciously provided to shield my sleeping bag from the dirt floor for the few days I would be a visitor in his house.

"We hear a lot about your country nowadays. But that has only been for the last fifteen years or so. Before then we never heard of your place. We heard about Iran and Germany and England—you know, where Peshawar is—and Russia . . . and China, but not about America. It must be far away. How long did it take you to get here? A week! Did you come by boat or by bus? By airplane! And it took you a week?" He sighed with amazement.

"Well," I said, "we weren't traveling all that time. We stopped along the way for two or three days in a couple of places."

"Ho! So far!" The further clarification was no help.

He drew a long draft of air through his teeth, the way a peasant farmer does when he's about to say something serious. "They tell me there is a big river over there somewhere, you know, that you have to cross before you come here."

"A big river?"

"That's what I heard—is there a big river over there?"

"You mean a big, wide stretch of water, a whole lot of water?" I couldn't remember the Afghan Farsi word for "ocean."

He grunted his affirmation.

"Well, it's a lot of water, but it isn't a river because it isn't moving anywhere. I mean, it doesn't go anywhere, like the water does in a river."

"What does it do?"

"I guess it just sits there. Well . . . it's just there." I was stumped by my limitations in the language.

He seemed to ponder, blankly, to himself.

"Well, it isn't always necessarily quiet," I said. "The wind can blow and make it move around a lot" (I didn't know the word for "waves" either).

"My God! You Are a Mussulman Man Like Me!"

Suddenly I remembered the word for ocean: "It's a *bahr*," I said. It didn't help him; he lived in the mountains of a landlocked country that had scarce reason to deal with oceans, and it seemed to have no real significance to him. "River" (*daryā*) seemed to do just fine for him.

"So your country is covered with water," he said thoughtfully.

"No, no," I cut in impatiently, "there's water all around it, but of course it isn't on top of the country."

"Oh." He adjusted his crossed legs and changed the subject. "Do you have mountains like these?" I affirmed it was so.

"I hear that you water your crops with airplanes."

"No, no," again I interrupted, "we only spread medicine over the crops with planes; we don't water crops that way."

"So you just irrigate your fields like we do."

"Well, yes, sometimes, but most of our farming is dryland (*lalmi*)."

"Dryland? All that wheat that comes to our country is from dryland?" He adjusted his feet again and leaned back on the cushion. "People say you have a machine that cuts the wheat for you. ... It also threshes the wheat at the same time? ... So then all you have to do is throw it in the air to separate the chaff. The machine does that, too? Ho! Such a machine!

"How much could this machine harvest in one day? Our whole valley in one day? I wish our government would give us one. Why doesn't your government give us one?"

I evaded the question by explaining that in my country the government doesn't give the machine to people; the farmers buy it themselves. "How much do they cost?"

"I'm not a farmer, so I suppose it would cost, maybe, $4,000 dollars or more." (In 1967 dollars.)

"How much is that in rupas?"

"Maybe, about 32,000 rupas."

"So much money! I suppose that's even more than your women cost!"

"Oh, they don't cost anything. I mean we don't have to pay anything to the father for the girl."

He sat up, gaping. "They are free?"

"Yes, we don't even go to the parents. We talk directly to the girl and make the agreement face to face with her."

He collapsed back on his cushion. The look on his face seemed to indicate profound amazement.

"You mean you just talk to her and . . . that's all?" He was speaking softly. "You just decide to take the girl and you just do it?"

"Uh-huh."

"And then you are just man and wife? I mean she just goes home with you?"

"Well, no. Of course, we have to get married before we do that." (Again, this was 1967, and this was Afghanistan. I didn't mention "the new morality.")

"Get married. So you have to get married over there too? Well!" He sat up with renewed interest, adjusted his brightly embroidered skullcap, and peered wide-eyed into my face. "You have to tell other people, right?"

"Yes, we call our mullah and he marries the boy and girl."

"You have a mullah? And he marries you! What do you know! You have a mullah! What does he do? Does he say something?"

"Well, he prays and . . ."

"He prays?" he interrupted with a start. "Your mullahs pray?"

"Of course they do!" I was offended.

"What do you know. . . . Wallah [By God!], sir, I didn't know!" He clapped his hand on the calf of his leg. "A guy would never know. I mean . . . if I hadn't talked to you. . . . Well, do you pray? I mean, do you pray too, or is it just the mullah?"

"Yes, of course, we pray too."

"What do you do? Do you kneel and bow, do you do rakas [prostrations] like we do?"

"No, we don't pray quite like you do."

"How often do you have to pray?"

"We don't have to pray any set number of times. We don't have rules like that."

"No rules?" He was not impressed.

I thought I had to explain. "What I mean is we believe that God has given us salvation as a gift so we don't have any rules except to love him with all our heart and to love each other."

"You don't have to do anything." He was having trouble understanding. "Do you have a prophet? We believe in 124,000 prophets, have you heard that?"

"Yes." I wanted to move to safer ground. "We are free to consider what we believe and to believe what we like. I believe in Jesus."

"In Jesus! Well, so do we! Sir, if I hadn't talked to you I wouldn't have known. So you Americans believe in Jesus!"

"Oh no, not all Americans. We are free to believe in Jesus or not to, as we like."

"Believe as you like, huh?" He drew his feet up into a squat, swiped his face with the back of his hand. He wasn't impressed.

I tried to explain. "We think it is better for people to be free to believe as they want—I mean we don't think people are worshipping if they are forced to worship in a certain way."

"You don't have to do anything and you don't have to believe anything." Now he was really unimpressed.

I tried to clarify. "Well, if we follow Jesus we have to believe something, but we don't force other people to believe what we believe, because we don't call it true faith if it doesn't come from within."

"It has to come from within." He seemed to ponder the idea tolerantly. Then he exclaimed, "By God, Sir, you are a *musulmān* man!" The word *musulmān* means a Muslim, a person who submits to the will of God (Arabic /s.l.m/ "submit"), but here it had the sense of an upright man who believed in God and submitted to him. "Sir," he said, "You are a *musulmān* man, like me."

"Yes," I said. "I am a *musulmān* man like you."

Our conversation was at that moment interrupted. Anyway, it seemed to reach an end point when Khodāhdād saw something in me that he could relate to. I was upright like him, he had decided, even if I was not a Muslim. He took me to be a *musulmān* man in the sense that like him I was a man of faith and good will. That was enough for him.

THE ETHNOGRAPHIC PROJECT

His discovery was, in a sense, my discovery too. I enjoyed coming to know him as a person of good will like myself. Coming from our different social backgrounds, and despite our different grounds of truth and reality, and the odd beliefs and practices he had heard about from me, he and I could accept each other as morally analogous to ourselves. We had a common ground of mutual empathy.

Ethnography aspires to understand the social lives of others. We perform our tasks, as best we can, seeking to be as empathetic as possible. For some of us, says the philosophical anthropologist Michael Jackson, ethnographic work can be a kind of controlled experiment on ourselves in hopes of "enlarging our understanding of what it means to be human." It enables us to see ourselves in the other, "as one might be or might have been under other circumstances." The reward for our projects is an ability to perceive ourselves in the "other." It is a perception unlike what we normally call "science." "Much as we try to name, contain, and control our interactions with the world around us," says Jackson, "the interplay between self and other has a life of its own." In that interplay, relationship can become fellowship, mutual enjoyment, in which we recognize each other's respective "moral personhood."[6] This is what David Pocock calls "the significance and . . . joy of human existence."[7] Whatever I was to Khodāhdād before we talked—*Khāreji? Kāfir?*—he now believed that I had a moral sensibility more or less like his own. I was, in his elegant Islamic vocabulary, a *musulmān* man like him.

---

6. Jackson, *Palm at the End*, 232–33. In chapter 10 of *The Listening Ebony*, Wendy James points out that the many differences in moral belief and practice among human beings mask a shared commonality of moral sentiments. I take this to be axiomatic.

7. Pocock, "Ethnography," 5.

"MY GOD! YOU ARE A MUSSULMAN MAN LIKE ME!"

KHODĀHDĀD IN THE BIBLE

How can we see Khodāhdād in the Biblical context? Someone like him was Abimelek, king of Gerar, who behaved honorably before God. When Abraham brought his flocks into the Negev, a region new to him, he lied about the identity of Sarah who, he knew, would be sought after because of her beauty. He let out that she was not his wife but his sister for fear that a local warlord would kill him for her. And indeed a local "king" named Abimelek took her into his harem. However, God warned Abimelek in a dream that he had no right to Sarah and was subject to destruction. Abimelek defended himself: "Lord, will you destroy an innocent nation? Did he not say to me, 'She is my sister,' and didn't she also say, 'He is my brother'? I have done this with a clear conscience and clean hands." God said, "Yes, I know you did this with a clear conscience."

The next day, when Abimelek challenged Abraham for lying to him, he explained that he had supposed, "There is surely no fear of God in this place, and they will kill me because of my wife."[8] So he lied to protect himself, supposing that the people in this strange land did not "fear God" and so might kill for his wife. In the conversation between Khodāhdād and me, that question whether I feared God infused the whole situation—or rather, which of us was the true fearer of God.

The gospel is that Christ died for the sins of the world.[9] That means for everyone. Even if people never hear about it, it's still good news. For those who have "never heard" as well as for us who have heard, the atoning work of Christ opened the door for God to show compassion to the upright in heart, in any society, in any age. The whole agenda of the sufferings of Christ was to open the way for people like Abimelek and Khodāhdād to approach God and love him and rejoice in him; as the Shorter Westminster Catechism says, "To glorify God and enjoy him forever."[10] Of course, like the rest of us they didn't deserve his mercy, and like everyone

---

8. Gen 20:1–11.
9. 1 John 2:2.
10. Westminster Standard, "Shorter Catechism," Q&A 1.

they didn't earn it. If they enjoyed God's mercy, it is because the God who searches every heart knew their earnest intention to follow God's laws as they best knew them. As Abimelek said to God, he had acted sincerely; what he did was appropriate as far as he knew. And his sincerity was acknowledged by God.

The One who would be the judge of all human beings taught that, "from everyone who has been given much, much will be demanded; and from the one who has been entrusted with much, much more will be asked."[11] This is why we can believe that, as Professor Piper put it, "No one will be judged for not obeying revelation they did not have. We will all be judged according to the knowledge of the truth we have access to. All of us, every human being on the planet, has access . . . to the knowledge of God."[12] And to that degree everyone is accountable to him. This merciful God, in any case, knew that everyone would be helpless before his judgment, and in one decisive moral act gave himself to pay for all the wickedness in human history, and, as the writer of Hebrews says, destroyed the power of the devil, the fountain of evil.[13]

Taking Khodāhdād as a moral type of human being, we can regard him as like Abimelek and Abraham, but in different ways. He was like Abimelek in that he and Abimelek seemed to be trying to behave correctly before God. They were upright human beings. And in the case of Abimelek, God acknowledged it. In the end, the One who knows every heart will judge each of them (including mine) according to what they knew about his laws. But Khodāhdād was also like Abraham in supposing that the *khāreji* he had just met had "no fear of God" as he did. As he said himself in our conversation, he discovered otherwise. And I take his acknowledgment of me as a supreme compliment.

---

11. Luke 12:48.
12. Piper, "We Are Accountable," para. 13.
13. Heb 2:14–17.

10

The Authority of Twelve Jewish Men

It is necessary to choose one of the men who
have been with us the whole time.[1]

FROM VERY EARLY IN Jesus's career, people debated who he was and what he was doing. Rumors about him proliferated. The Gospel of John says this about the rumors:

> On hearing his words, some of the people said, "Surely this man is the Prophet."
> Others said, "He is the Messiah." Still others asked, "How can the Messiah come from Galilee? Does not Scripture say that the Messiah will come from David's descendants and from Bethlehem, the town where David lived?" Thus, the people were divided because of Jesus. Some wanted to seize him, but no one laid a hand on him.[2]

---

1. Acts 1:21.
2. John 7:40–44.

Walking Blind

It was to counter the rumors and debates about him that Jesus chose twelve men to follow him, to hear his teachings to the crowds, see his marvelous works, and give a united witness about him once he was gone. This was their importance. Before he left he commissioned them to tell his story, what he had done, what he had taught, and especially to testify to the reality of his resurrection: "You will receive power when the Holy Spirit comes on you; and you will be my witnesses in Jerusalem, and in all Judea and Samaria, and to the ends of the earth."[3]

Why twelve? Why not ten? Or seven? Or why a specific number of disciples at all? Almost immediately Jesus had a crowd following him; "large crowds" followed him, say the Gospel writers.[4] There was a reason for choosing twelve individuals to train more fully than all the rest.

The number twelve is notable in the Semite tradition. Ishmael was the father of "twelve rulers," Jacob the father of twelve sons.[5] The number twelve was reflected in many collective activities of the Israelites. Twelve fresh loaves of unleavened bread were placed in the tabernacle every week.[6] Twelve stones were sewed into the breastplate of the high priest's garment.[7] Twelve men were sent to spy out the land of Canaan.[8] When the people of Israel crossed the Jordan River, they collected twelve stones from the middle of the river and piled them into a memorial mound on the other side at the point where the tabernacle first touched the land of Canaan.[9] Solomon appointed twelve officers over Israel.[10] Elijah built an altar of twelve stones when he called fire down from heaven.[11]

---

3. Acts 1:8.
4. Matt 4:25.
5. Gen 17:20; 25:16.
6. Lev 24:5–7.
7. Exod 28:21.
8. Num 13.
9. Josh 4:3.
10. 1 Kgs 4:7.
11. 1 Kgs 18:31.

The Authority of Twelve Jewish Men

So what could the number twelve signify? One biblical commentator has suggested that the number stands for something like "completeness."[12]

Jesus seems to have chosen twelve disciples so that they could be a body of individuals large enough to give substantial proof to the stories that they would tell about him: what he said, what he did, and eventually that he rose from the grave. These declarations were to be made by the twelve men. It was a way to ensure that the stories they would tell about him could be trusted as "true," authentic events in Jesus's life, to counter the rumors that would inevitably circulate among the people. Much has been made of how diverse the twelve were. It included Matthew, who had been a tax collector for the Romans; and Simon the Zealot who had belonged to the movement seeking to drive the Romans out of the country. I wonder if this assemblage of characters could have reflected the diverse perspectives of people in Judah at that time. At least they seem to have been men of opinions, and ready to declare them. They quarreled over which one was greatest.[13]

But by the time that they would see Jesus for the last time they were different men. They had been with Jesus in many settings, seen his works, heard his teachings, shared private moments with him. And most memorably, they had witnessed his betrayal, seen his pain as virtually everyone around, including themselves, abandoned him. One of them, one of their original number, betrayed him, and they themselves had fled when a mob seized him and dragged him away to be tried and condemned to death by his enemies. Those twelve chosen men had stood at a distance to watch silently as Jesus suffered his last hours, jeered by the crowds and taunted by the chief priests. The horror of what they experienced traumatized them, and they were mortified by their own cowardice. The total collapse of all that they had confidently believed left them dismayed, confused, and helpless.

The day after the crucifixion was also awful. They hid away in fear. Did any of them remember that he had told them he would

12. Lee, "What Should We Know."
13. Mark 9:34.

be killed? Even though they were told several times that he would die and rise again, they could not conceive of his rising from death. Resurrection from death—that death!—was unthinkable. Everything was a fog. What would happen next? Would the chief priests come after them too?

The second morning after the crucifixion began with the startling news by some of the women who had breathlessly declared that the tomb was empty. They didn't believe them. The body had disappeared? What could have happened? When Jesus appeared to them and upbraided them for their unbelief they were stunned but of course they were thrilled, overcome with joy. Now they were full of questions. Someone asked, "Lord, are you at this time going to restore the kingdom to Israel?" and Jesus told them, "It is not for you to know the times or dates the Father has set by his own authority. But you will receive power when the Holy Spirit comes on you; and you will be my witnesses in Jerusalem, and in all Judea and Samaria, and to the ends of the earth."[14] And soon he was gone.

Now what?

He had told them to wait in the city until they would be "clothed with power from on high," another saying they did not understand.[15] As they waited, they organized. For them the absence of Judas was a troubling vacancy. His place needed to be filled.[16] Peter took the initiative. Referring to a line in Ps 109, "May another take his place of leadership," he proposed that they add someone to their number. "Therefore," he said, "it is necessary to choose one of the men who have been with us the whole time the Lord Jesus was living among us, beginning from John's baptism to the time when Jesus was taken up from us. For one of these must become a witness with us of his resurrection."[17] So they cast lots, and the person chosen, Matthias, joined the twelve to become an official witness of Christ's resurrection. Now their number was complete. None of them could have known how quickly they

---

14. Acts 1:6–8.
15. Luke 24:49.
16. Acts 1:20.
17. Acts 1:21–22.

would be put to work testifying many things about Jesus. They would soon be caught up in activities that would carry them, as Jesus told them, to places beyond their horizons, where they would testify of his resurrection.

As they prayed and waited, on the day of Pentecost, seven weeks after the previous Passover period when Jesus had been killed, entombed, and rose, the twelve and other early believers were together when Luke says, "They saw what seemed to be tongues of fire that separated and came to rest on each of them."[18] The Holy Spirit came upon them and produced in them praises of the Lord in various languages. And also the sound of a powerful wind swirled around them. The sound and the voices exclaiming the praises of God in several languages reached the ears of neighbors and the news ramified out into the city. The sense that something strange was happening drew people from the city to come looking, wanting to find out what was going on. In the midst of the commotion the twelve began to explain what was happening. Peter rose up to get the attention of the crowd. He explained that what they were seeing and hearing was the fulfillment of a prophesy of the ancient prophet Joel:

> In the last days, God says, I will pour out my Spirit on all people. Your sons and daughters will prophesy, your young men will see visions, your old men will dream dreams. Even on my servants, both men and women, I will pour out my Spirit in those days, and they will prophesy. I will show wonders in the heavens above and signs on the earth below, blood and fire and billows of smoke. The sun will be turned to darkness and the moon to blood before the coming of the great and glorious day of the Lord. And everyone who calls on the name of the Lord will be saved.[19]

Peter linked this dramatic moment with the terrible events of the recent Passover.

---

18. Luke 2:3.
19. Acts 2:17–21.

> Fellow Israelites, I can tell you confidently that the patriarch David died and was buried, and his tomb is here to this day. But he was a prophet and knew that God had promised him an oath that he would place one of his descendants on his throne. Seeing what was to come, he spoke of the resurrection of the Messiah, that he was not abandoned to the realm of the dead, nor did his body see decay. God has raised this Jesus to life, and we are all witnesses of it. Exalted to the right hand of God, he has received from the Father the promised Holy Spirit and has poured out what you now see and hear.[20]

And after quoting one of the Messianic promises in the Psalms he concluded, "Therefore let all Israel be assured of this: God has made this Jesus, whom you crucified, both Lord and Messiah."[21]

The Jews who had gathered in the city had come from many places—Luke says "from every nation under heaven"—to celebrate the feast of Pentecost. They were stunned by Peter's challenge that the Messiah had come and been executed in the city, and they pled to know what they should do. "Repent and be baptized," said Peter, "every one of you, in the name of Jesus Christ for the forgiveness of your sins. And you will receive the gift of the Holy Spirit."[22] Peter's urging was supported by the voices of the other disciples and together they collectively gave witness to all that Peter had said. The body whose disappearance had flummoxed the notables had risen, they said. They had seen him and conversed with him, and also many other of his followers had seen him. The Messiah had come, they asserted. He had been rejected and executed, but on the third day he rose. The Messiah had come, and he was alive! They had seen him themselves and talked with him.

The united declarations of the twelve became the message that would awaken a movement of testimony and faith that spread quickly throughout the city. The men spoke with authority and recounted many experiences with Jesus, what he said, what he did.

20. Acts 2:29–33.
21. Acts 2:36.
22. Acts 2:38.

As a result, hundreds of the people who had gathered in the city to celebrate the Passover embraced the "good news" that the Messiah had come and had risen from death. The testimonies of these twelve men at that strategic moment provided the basis for the spread of the proclamation that would emanate from Jerusalem to neighboring cities, eventually to the world: the Messiah had come.

Of course, the crowd surrounding the twelve wanted to know more. As their numbers grew into the thousands, from day to day they pressed the disciples—now apostles, the "sent ones"—for ever more information, more stories about Jesus. William F. Albright and C. S. Mann remark on this period, "Because of the nature of the gospel proclamation, the original oral repetition of the story of Jesus and his teachings did not satisfy the early Christians for long."[23] The pressing need for information about Jesus soon induced those at the center of the movement to produce short written statements about specific events in Jesus's life that could be copied and shared among the believers. This was the setting in which many pericopes (from the Greek for a small block of written material) about Jesus appeared in the community. Eventually, many pericopes about what he did and said were being circulated. These pericopes included the story of the feeding of five thousand, feeding the four thousand, the lost sheep, the lost coin, the raising of the daughter of Jairus, the centurion who asked for his servant to be healed, the woman caught in adultery, the lecture on the signs of the last age, and so on.[24] As more and more such stories were written down, presumably authorized (if not written) by the twelve, these pericopes seem to have been gathered into a corpus of written materials about Jesus that were recognized by the community of believers.[25] They may have been assembled to be useful for instructing new believers. A set of pericopes may have been "at a very early stage a kind of catechists' manual, which was used to

---

23. Albright and Mann, *Matthew*, xxii.

24. See chapter 3.

25. This collection of notes about Jesus's life are now called Q, which stands for "Quelle," the German word for source.

provide tested and approved answers to questions."[26] Later, when the writers of the Synoptic Gospels set out to tell the story of Jesus to their respective audiences, they drew from this body of written materials.[27]

The movement that declared that this Jesus, "a man accredited by God . . . by miracles, wonders and signs," was distinctive for its annunciation ("Jesus has risen from the dead!") and for its promise ("Jesus is coming back to judge of the world!"). The twelve were the source of these claims, and they would carry their message to a widening circle of peoples and nations. As the twelve scattered far and wide, each one persisted in announcing to his death that he had himself known the risen Jesus after his sufferings, and he had conversed with him for some days after his resurrection.

Here was the importance of the twelve. They testified as a group and also, after they had dispersed, as individuals. They brought the testimony that Jesus the Messiah had come, been crucified, risen, to faraway places, authorizing their claims by a zeal that carried most of them, in the face of all opposition, to their deaths. They were urgent in their appeals to repent, for they believed that Jesus, in fulfillment of Joel's prophesy, would soon return to judge the world.

Twelve men.

When else has a group of twelve Jewish men agreed on anything so momentous?

---

26. Albright and Mann, *Matthew*, xxiv.

27. Most of the writings in the New Testament were written before the Romans attacked Jerusalem in AD 70.

11

The Greatest Social Critics of All Time

> All are greedy for gain. Prophets and priests alike, all practice deceit.
> ...Are they ashamed of their loathsome conduct? No, they have no shame. They do not know how to blush.[1]

PEOPLE WHO ARE UNFAMILIAR with the Bible suppose that the Old Testament prophets only prophesied. It's true; many of them did foretell events in significant ways. But most of them were preeminently social critics, especially of the leadership of their societies. And they were especially critical of the religious leaders of their time.

Many of them were rejected during their own times. Jeremiah was of course the most notable of them to be persecuted: he was flogged at least twice, he was placed under house arrest, he was put in the stocks, and dumped in a well. Without some loyal friends he

---

1. Jer 8:10, 12.

would have died—and indeed, the last we know of him is that he was dragged away to Egypt against his will.

What he had to say was regarded by officials as treason, and if some had had their way he would have been formally executed. Other prophets as far as we can tell were, if not persecuted, then ignored—often only tolerated. What they all shared was a definite sense that God was in charge of history; and they spoke in his name.

So what was it that made them so offensive? It was what they had to say about the leaders of their times, especially the religious figures, whose power was formidable in their society. The prophets, despite their individual limitations in social leverage, exerted their impact by describing social situations and the behavior of their leaders in virulent, vivid, sometimes even grotesque terms. Ezekiel's vocabulary and imagery were so gross, so sexually explicit, in their allegorical description of Israel's betrayal of God, that in later generations some Jews refused to read it aloud in the synagogues. (The offending passage deserves a separate discussion; it is one of the most deeply moving passages in the Bible for those of us who, like the Israelites, have betrayed our God.)

Here I merely point out how vivid and pointed are the critical images that the prophets created about leaders and societies who were offending God. Always—and this is what those who know nothing of the Bible are unprepared for—the corrections they call for, are critiques for social reforms: provisioning the poor, care for the "fatherless," the widow, and the alien. Here are some examples.

From Jeremiah:

> From the least to the greatest, all are greedy for gain; prophets and priests alike, all practice deceit. They dress the wound of my people as though it were not serious. "Peace, peace," they say, when there is no peace. Are they ashamed of their loathsome conduct? No, they have no shame; they do not even know how to blush.[2]

---

2. Jer 6:13–15.

> Can an Ethiopian change his skin or a leopard its spots? Neither can you do good who are accustomed to doing evil.[3]

> "Woe to the shepherds who are destroying and scattering the sheep of my pasture!" declares the LORD. Therefore this is what the LORD, the God of Israel, says to the shepherds who tend my people: "Because you have scattered my flock and driven them away and have not bestowed care on them, I will bestow punishment on you for the evil you have done," declares the LORD. "I myself will gather the remnant of my flock out of all the countries where I have driven them and will bring them back to their pasture, where they will be fruitful and increase in number. I will place shepherds over them who will tend them, and they will no longer be afraid or terrified, nor will any be missing," declares the LORD.[4]

From Isaiah:

> When you come to appear before me, who has asked this of you, this trampling of my courts? Stop bringing meaningless offerings! Your incense is detestable to me. New Moons, Sabbaths and convocations—I cannot bear your evil assemblies. Your New Moon festivals and your appointed feasts my soul hates. They have become a burden to me; I am weary of bearing them. When you spread out your hands in prayer, I will hide my eyes from you. Even if you offer many prayers, I will not listen. Your hands are full of blood; wash and make yourselves clean. Take your evil deeds out of my sight! Stop doing wrong, learn to do right! Seek justice. Encourage the oppressed. Defend the cause of the fatherless. Plead the case of the widow.[5]

> Declare to my people their rebellion.... For day after day they seek me out; they seem eager to know my ways, as if they were a nation that does what is right and has not forsaken the commands of its God. They ask me for just

---

3. Jer 13:23.
4. Jer 23:1–4.
5. Isa 1:12–17.

decisions and seem eager for God to come near them. "Why have we fasted," they say, "and you have not seen it? Why have we humbled ourselves, and you have not noticed?" Yet on the day of your fasting, you do as you please and exploit all your workers. Your fasting ends in quarreling and strife. . . . You cannot fast as you do today and expect your voice to be heard on high. Is this the kind of fast I have chosen, only a day for people to humble themselves? Is it only for bowing one's head like a reed and for lying in sackcloth and ashes? Is that what you call a fast, a day acceptable to the LORD? Is not this the kind of fasting I have chosen: to loose the chains of injustice and untie the cords of the yoke, to set the oppressed free and break every yoke? Is it not to share your food with the hungry and to provide the poor wanderer with shelter—when you see the naked, to clothe them, and not to turn away from your own flesh and blood? . . . If you do away with the yoke of oppression, with the pointing finger and malicious talk, and if you spend yourselves on behalf of the hungry and satisfy the needs of the oppressed, then your light will rise in the darkness, and your night will become like the noonday.[6]

From Micah:

Woe to those who plan iniquity, to those who plot evil on their beds! At morning's light they carry it out because it is in their power to do it. They covet fields and seize them, and houses, and take them. They defraud a man of his home, a fellowman of his inheritance. Therefore, the LORD says: "I am planning disaster against this people, from which you cannot save yourselves. You will no longer walk proudly, for it will be a time of calamity. In that day men will ridicule you; they will taunt you with this mournful song: 'We are utterly ruined; my people's possession is divided up. He takes it from me! He assigns our fields to traitors.'"[7]

---

6. Isa 58:1–10. This portion of Isaiah is believed by many scholars to have been written after the time of Isaiah of Jerusalem and is therefore according to Second Isaiah.

7. Mic 2:1–4.

The Greatest Social Critics of All Time

From Ezekiel:

Son of man, prophesy against the shepherds of Israel; prophesy and say to them: "This is what the Sovereign Lord says: Woe to the shepherds of Israel who only take care of themselves! Should not shepherds take care of the flock? You eat the curds, clothe yourselves with the wool and slaughter the choice animals, but you do not take care of the flock. You have not strengthened the weak or healed the sick or bound up the injured. You have not brought back the strays or searched for the lost. You have ruled them harshly and brutally. So they were scattered because there was no shepherd, and when they were scattered, they became food for all the wild animals. My sheep wandered over all the mountains and on every high hill. They were scattered over the whole earth, and no one searched or looked for them. Therefore, you shepherds, hear the word of the Lord: As surely as I live, declares the Sovereign Lord, because my flock lacks a shepherd and so has been plundered and has become food for all the wild animals, and because my shepherds did not search for my flock but cared for themselves rather than for my flock, therefore, O shepherds, hear the word of the Lord: . . . I am against the shepherds and will hold them accountable for my flock. I will remove them from tending the flock so that the shepherds can no longer feed themselves. I will rescue my flock from their mouths, and it will no longer be food for them. For this is what the Sovereign Lord says: I myself will search for my sheep and look after them. As a shepherd looks after his scattered flock when he is with them, so will I look after my sheep. I will rescue them from all the places where they were scattered on a day of clouds and darkness. I will bring them out from the nations and gather them from the countries, and I will bring them into their own land. I will pasture them on the mountains of Israel, in the ravines and in all the settlements in the land. I will tend them in a good pasture, and the mountain heights of Israel will be their grazing land. There they will lie down in good grazing land, and there they will feed in a rich pasture on the mountains of Israel. I myself will tend my sheep and have them lie down, declares the Sovereign LORD. I will search for the lost and bring back the strays. I will bind up the injured and strengthen the weak, but the sleek and the strong I will destroy. I will shepherd the flock with justice."[8]

From Malachi (in the voice of Yahweh):

"My covenant was with [Levi], a covenant of life and peace, and I gave them to him. This called for reverence and he revered me and stood in awe of my name. True instruction was in his mouth and nothing false was found on his lips. He walked with me in peace and uprightness, and turned many from sin. For the lips of a priest ought to preserve knowledge, and from his mouth men should seek instruction—because he is the messenger of the LORD Almighty. But you have turned from the way and by your teaching have caused many to stumble; you have violated the covenant with Levi," says the LORD Almighty. "So I have caused you to be despised and humiliated before all the people, because you have not followed my ways but have shown partiality in matters of the law."[9]

---

8. Ezek 34:2–16.
9. Mal 2:5–9.

12

The Bang and the Glory

In the beginning God created the heavens and the earth.[1]

IF ANY VERSE IN the Bible is well known, this has to be it. I suppose that many people think this is the way the Bible talks. Many people seem never to explore beyond the first two chapters of Genesis. It's what they are missing that prompts my ventures of textual explication here.

The verse is also one of the most discussed verses in the Bible. Many of my Christian friends are so occupied with the miraculous work of God as the creator, as described here, that they bristle at any discussion of the mechanisms entailed in the creative act. They surmise nothing more can be said about creation. To them the miracle is somehow denied by discussions of the material processes that take place in nature, or might have taken place in the past. Some of my friends claim to distrust "science." At the same time they want medical care to reflect the best knowledge of the

---

1. Gen 1:1.

field. That the whole edifice of scientific thought rests on the same assumptions escapes them.

It seems to me that those who take this view may misunderstand the nature of science, so I here briefly seek to clarify what science is and is not. Science is an attempt to understand the universe in its own terms. True, it took generations of argumentation and dispute to reach agreement on how the natural world could be examined for its internal workings, but as science now exists its categories and measurements are necessarily grounded in the mechanisms of the natural world.

What we call science was at one time called "natural philosophy" to distinguish the rational inquiry of the empirical world from the more abstract "philosophy" that flourished after the discovery, or rediscovery, of Greek philosophical thought in the twelfth and thirteenth centuries. The focus of natural philosophy was partly driven by the remarkable flood of new information into Europe after the rise of world maritime trade and the "age of discovery" that began to flourish in the sixteenth century. The focus shifted to understanding the material world being discovered in so many forms.

Francis Bacon (1561–1626) thought that in championing empirical enquiry he had made a contribution to natural philosophy. Isaac Newton (1643–1727) called his famous book *Mathematical Principles of Natural Philosophy*. Newton formulated not only the principles of how physical bodies relate to each other but also the mathematics of those relations, and so inspired a quest among other scientists to discover more laws operative in the natural world.

A fundamental concept of geological and astronomical thought we call "uniformitarianism." The Scottish geologist James Hutton (1726–1797) didn't use the word but the concept was implied in his 1785 paper claiming that the earth's long history could be inferred from processes going on in the present. His argument was promoted by Sir Charles Lyell (1797–1875) and finally given its name by William Whewell in 1832.

And from such assumptions the twentieth century produced a marvel of scientific conceptions that bears on our understanding of the opening words of Genesis. The concept that all matter actually burst out from a single point at some time in the astronomical past—the instant of "creation"—was formulated in 1927 by the Catholic priest and mathematician Georges Lemaître. Lemaître developed his "hypothesis of the primeval atom" out of Albert Einstein's concept of general relativity, making use of general equations formulated by Alexander Friedmann.

A mere two years later, Edwin Hubble, peering into the heavens, discovered that the distances of galaxies were generally proportional to the red shift of light they emitted, suggesting that they were moving away from our galaxy—in fact, faster the further away they were. Galaxies seemed to be bursting out from a single point, suggesting that the universe was continually expanding, and in all directions. From this conception arose the proposal that at one time all matter must have burst from a single point.

Fred Hoyle, who at the time was scornful of the concept, in a 1949 radio broadcast gave us the elegantly graphic term "big bang" for this concept. And in 1965, Arno Penzias and Robert Wilson, to their own surprise, discovered cosmic microwave background radiation that seemed to provide incontrovertible evidence of the big bang. Scientists now, after applying various measurements, have agreed that the fateful moment, the explosive beginning of all beginnings, took place about 13.79 billion years ago. Such a concept, simply inconceivable in the nineteenth century, has become standard scientific thought in the twenty-first.

But this is not the focus of the Bible. Here the preeminent concern is with God as the magnificent independent figure who stands outside of and beyond the universe he created. The psalmist formulates the real orientation of the Bible: "The heavens declare the glory of God and the earth shows his handiwork."[2] What the scientist sees as natural forms driven by powerful and ineluctable forces, the psalmist sees as "the glory of God" and "the handiwork of God." The science of the universe, a construction of formulations always subject to review and revision, is not contrary to the

2. Ps 19:1.

preoccupation of the Bible but complementary to it. Science is another way of knowing.

Those of us with scientific interests are discovering something of how God did what he did and does what he does, but there is no necessary compromise with the notion that God has projects unexaminable in uniformitarian terms of science. Voltaire usefully proposed that a "philosophy of history" (the study of human beings and their affairs) is possible even if we cannot know what God is doing in the world; a science of the human condition can be pursued without reference to the providence of God. Whatever God is doing in the world, it escapes our quest to develop rational understandings of human society and the human condition.

The focus of the Bible and of the book of Genesis is the God who created everything known and knowable. He is its central figure, its hero. It indicates that he has plans and projects in the world among the human beings he created. God has revealed himself, some of it, to human beings. He is not only a creator—this, many texts of the Bible collectively assume, imply, and affirm—but he is also a personality whose opinions directly bear on the behavior and affairs of human beings on earth. Those things we can learn from the Bible.

The Bible begins with the declaration, "God created the heavens and the earth." Precisely how he did it, what the material mechanisms of that creative instant were—such issues will continue to vex scientists as long as rational thought exists. In the meantime, along with the psalmist those of us who are believers allow ourselves to marvel at the glory of his creative work. Some years ago I was deeply moved by a photograph of the Horsehead Nebula by Adam Block.[3] But since then we have all been dazzled by the images of the James Webb Space Telescope. And even more ambitious devices for viewing the sky are in the works.

How can we look out into the universe through these amazing modern devices and not be in awe!

---

3. See Block, "Horsehead Nebula."

Lift up your eyes and look to the heavens: Who created all these?[4]

Two things fill the mind with ever new and increasing admiration and awe ... the starry heavens above and the moral law within.[5]

---

4. Isa 40:26.
5. Kant, *Critique of Practical Reason*, loc. 2797.

13

A Strange Prophetic Sign of the World in Crisis

WE TEND TO EMPHASIZE passages in the Bible that suit our preferences and overlook others that don't. The Beatitudes for instance. These appear as the opening lines of what we now call the Sermon on the Mount, a sermon that appears only in Matthew's Gospel. A portion of it appears in Luke's Gospel, but Mark's Gospel makes no mention of it. There is, at the same time, another sermon, probably more of a lecture than a sermon, that appears in all three Synoptic Gospels, now referred to as the Olivet Discourse. All three Gospel writers provide long quotations from that discourse. Clearly the writers of the Synoptic Gospels saw this as a defining feature of Jesus's message.

A strange verse appears in Luke's version of this lecture, not reproduced in any other Gospel, that I have wondered about for years. As for many of the verses in the Bible that pique my curiosity, I have never heard a sermon on it. I've never heard anyone even bring it up as an issue.

> On the earth, nations will be in anguish and perplexity
> at the roaring and tossing of the sea. Men will faint from
> terror, apprehensive of what is coming on the world, for
> the heavenly bodies will be shaken.[1]

The very next verse is, "At that time they will see the Son of Man coming in a cloud with power and great glory." The implication is that the roaring and tossing of the sea is a preliminary indication of Christ's coming.

It is not unusual for people to take an interest in the final few words of this statement: "The heavenly bodies will be shaken," and, of course, "At that time they will see the Son of Man coming." On the other hand, I have never heard any discussion about the prophecy that nations will be "in anguish and perplexity at the roaring and tossing of the sea."

What kind of situation would bring about the roaring and tossing of the sea? The text suggests a world catastrophe that is pervasive, general, of even "biblical" proportions. Ezekiel refers to the four "dreadful judgments" of God: the sword, famine, wild beasts, and plague.[2] The book of Revelation refers to four dreadful horsemen: one that conquers, one that spreads internecine conflict, one that spreads famine, and one that is given the power to kill by sword, famine, plague, and wild beasts.[3] Unimaginable images for many of us.

But the world we can imagine in our time seems, on many counts, to be careening out of control. So, where is the world going? As we peer into the fog of the future we wonder if we are seeing developments that make this strange verse seem possible. Some experts predict that pandemics will become more common. Some are at this time of writing expressing concern about what the technology of war will be like, once AI computing becomes more refined. And of course I hardly need to refer to political issue engrossing the world to awaken the angst of a frightening future felt among growing numbers of people. So our imagination generates

1. Luke 21:25–26.
2. Ezek 14:21.
3. Rev 6:1–8.

many worrying possibilities that were unthinkable only a few years ago.

Figure 4. Global Land-Ocean Temperature Index[4]

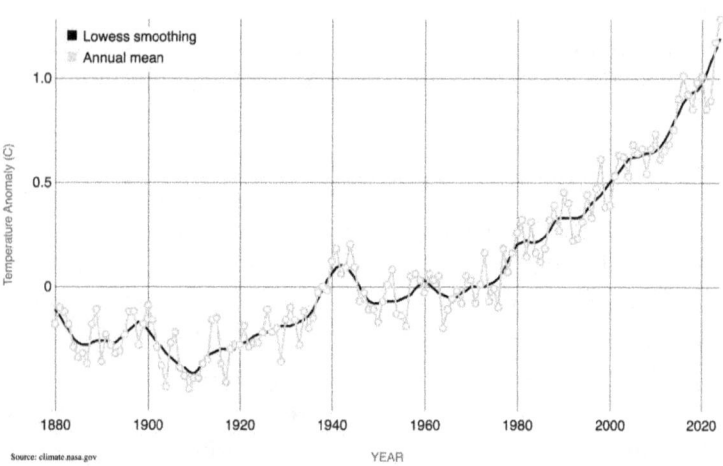

Source: climate.nasa.gov

Is the climate of the Earth on the verge of a major "tipping point," as some affirm? The debate about global warming—now called climate change—is driven by the rising sense of urgency among climate scientists about what is coming upon the earth. Even though climate warming has lately been a political flash point, it is actually not new. As far back as thirty-five years ago one of my colleagues showed me a graph of the amounts of CO_2 levels at various times over the last several thousand years, based on ice cores taken from the Greenland icecap. The sharp rise in CO_2 levels that began early in the twentieth century and then rose dramatically after 2000 seems easy enough to explain by the rising importance of the automobile in the twentieth century, which demanded escalating amounts of fossil fuels.

The consensus of the climate scientists is that the Earth is warming at an ever-faster pace. Some voices contest this concern but it turns out that they come from outside the scholarly circles

4. NASA/GISS, "Global Land-Ocean Temperature Index."

that specialize in global climate. Naomi Oreskes and Erik M. Conway call those voices "Merchants of Doubt."[5] Philip Kitcher summarizes their point in his review of climate change debates: "Opposition to scientifically well-supported claims about the dangers of cigarette smoking, the difficulties of the Strategic Defense Initiative ('Star Wars'), the effects of acid rain, the existence of the ozone hole, the problems caused by secondhand smoke, and—ultimately—the existence of anthropogenic climate change was used in 'the service of political goals and commercial interests' to obstruct the transmission of important information to the American public. Amazingly, the same small cadre of obfuscators figured in all these episodes."[6]

Oreskes and Conway discovered that scientists tied to particular industries, with strong political connections, have played a disproportionate role in debates about contested issues. Even though they obtained their stature in fields with little pertinence to the issues in question they posed as experts, many of them paid by think tanks devoted to contesting claims that threaten the interests of powerful corporations and political interests. The attempt has been to shape the way the public thinks about the natural processes that threaten the world, but it seems likely that any attempt to deny the processes of nature cannot prevail in the long run. The natural world operates according to its own mechanisms, whatever we think. The task of science of course is to faithfully seek an understanding of those mechanisms whatever they are. Obviously, if the climate experts are right, the earth is facing critical developments that will not go away.

What most climate scientists foresee is indeed reason to worry. If we consider how the dangerous trends in the world can be turned around, to turn back the trend of CO_2 production that is causing climate change, we find good reasons to consider the situation dire. That is, there are natural processes and there are social processes.

---

5. Oreskes and Conway, *Merchants of Doubt*.
6. Kitcher, "Climate Change Debates," 1233.

Anthony Giddens, the sociologist who has joined the debate, puts it this way: "It will be a colossal task to turn around a society whose whole way of life is constructed around mobility and a 'natural right' to consume energy in a profligate way."[7] A colossal task, yes. Turning around a civilization that is hell-bent on carrying on as it always has, driven by institutional conventions familiar and opulently funded, will indeed be a Herculean task. That the system in place denies any scientific findings that threaten its existence should be no surprise, for it is constituted to protect its own interests.

So why does Giddens add the following codicil to his elegantly formulated assertion: "Yet it isn't as hopeless an endeavor as it looks"? Did Giddens reach for a straw to avoid admitting how unlikely it is for the modern world to rise to the challenge of global warming? It seems obvious enough that what is actually required for the world to transform itself is a massive reconstitution of itself. So how likely is that? It is minimal. Is the reality too hideous for Giddens to put it into words?

I have referred to Giddens merely as an illustration of the problem we are all have in trying talk about the problem without seeming totally without hope. Robert N. Stavins, A. J. Meyer Professor of Energy and Economic Development, Harvard Kennedy School of Government, has expressed the problem clearly and simply. "The most severe consequences of climate change will be in the long term. But climate-change policies and the attendant costs of mitigation will be up front. This combination of up-front costs and delayed benefits presents a tremendous political challenge, since political incentives in democracies are typically for elected officials to convey benefits to current voters today, and place costs on future generations. The climate problem asks politicians to do precisely the opposite!"[8]

This is the context in which the predictions of Jesus in the verse at hand seem intelligible and of contemporary interest. Shifting our focus from the reality we can clearly foresee to the prophecy of Jesus, I wonder if our world could be on the verge of seeing

---

7. Giddens, *Politics of Climate Change*, 229.
8. Quoted in Mineo, "What Scares You Most," para. 27.

what Jesus prophesied. Could it take place before our eyes? Jesus's prophecy seems to imply that at some future point the world will suffer a general catastrophe. There will be a no-turning-back point, it suggests, when all reasonable hope of reversing a global march to disaster will fade. At that point, when people lose all hope, it says, some folks will collapse into in despair. Could that be coming in my lifetime? Indeed, it is conceivable. Kitcher says that the disappointing results of the United Nations Climate Change Conference in Copenhagen in 2009 indicates that "the world is lapsing into a state of resignation."[9] Already some scientists doubt that the rising levels of global CO_2 can be reversed.

So, I wonder, is "the roaring and tossing of the sea" already inevitable? What has not happened, and may not take form for a good while (assuming all this is true), is a public awareness that such a serious situation looms before the world. We can expect, in any case, to hear about American ingenuity, one of the lies we tell ourselves; someone will find a way, it will be said. Like Anthony Giddens, some will insist to the very end on denying what they see; they will hold out every hope that the disaster may never come to pass.

There is another part of Jesus's prediction that doesn't seem thinkable in our time: the whole statement is, "Men will faint from terror, apprehensive of what is coming on the world, for the heavenly bodies will be shaken." What could "the heavenly bodies be shaken" mean? Actually, this statement is the third time in this passage that Jesus mentions portents in the heavens. In v. 11 he predicts "fearful events and great signs from heaven," and in v. 25 he refers to "signs in the sun, moon and stars."

These images—signs from heaven, signs in the sun, moon, and stars, heavenly bodies that are shaken—escape my imaginative capacity. No such things seem foreseeable to me. Like our former inability to imagine a rising sea and a heightening of the earth's cyclones I can't at this time picture how such things could take place. The roaring of the waves is conceivable in a warming world, but the rest of that predictive sentence seems beyond possibility. What could I be missing?

9. Kitcher, "Climate Change Debates," 1234.

14

Biblical Sources of the First Amendment

CHRISTIANITY IS THE NATIONAL RELIGION?

As THE UNITED STATES was being birthed, the Founding Fathers agreed to formally separate the rights of conscience from the political union they were trying to form. In our time, a sizeable number of Americans seem to be sympathetic to renouncing that agreement and instead want to make this country overtly and officially Christian.[1] Those who are deliberate in wanting to do this believe "that the American nation is defined by Christianity, and that the government should take active steps to keep it that way." They assert "that America is and must remain a 'Christian nation'—not merely as an observation about American history, but as a prescriptive program for what America must continue to be in the future."[2]

---

1. Ladner, "Quiet Rise."
2. Miller, "What Is Christian Nationalism."

The proportion of Americans who are inclined to such ideas is significant. Based on a survey in 2022 by the Public Religion Research Institute (PRRI),

- 27 percent of Americans are favorable to the idea of the US Government declaring that this is a Christian nation;
- 38 percent believe that "if the US moves away from our Christian foundations, we will not have a country anymore";
- 30 percent believe that "being Christian is an important part of being truly American";
- and 20 percent believe that "God has called Christians to exercise dominion over all areas of American society."[3]

THE STRUGGLE OVER STATE RELIGION

Evidently, some Americans have forgotten the reasons that this country, in its founding, broke from the long-established European tradition of merging religion and politics. The break from this view did not take place without conflict, even without persecution. And how people read the Bible had much to do with it. The settlers who founded colonies in America took it for granted in each case that the political community they were forming would have an official religion like the countries in Europe. Those who founded the Massachusetts Bay Colony assumed that their church was the official church of the colony. They presumed that the colony would enforce their religious teachings and rituals, as had been the case in England and elsewhere. In the 1630s, this idea was expressed by one of the most notable of their preachers, John Cotton. He declared that "the civil ruler had the duty to suppress ideas out of keeping with the 'right' religion" of the colony.[4]

---

3. "Christian Nation?" American people believe Christian nationalism is ascendant in this country. See Silver et al., *Comparing Levels*. See also Sumner, "Inside the Creepy Push" and Gedeon, "Trump's Taskforce Order."

4. Verduin, *Anatomy of a Hybrid*, 238.

There was, however, a question among some Christians about whether true faith could be enforced by government. They espoused the teachings of Jesus to "love the Lord your God with all your heart and with all your soul and with all your mind," and "to love your neighbor as yourself."[5] And they were reading the teachings of the apostle Paul, "Serve one another humbly in love."[6] And, "live by the Spirit," whose qualities he lists as "love, joy, peace, forbearance, kindness, goodness, faithfulness, gentleness and self-control,"[7] actions that can only come from a person willingly, from the heart. The folks who questioned whether authentic faith could be produced by law were influenced by these teachings.

The idea that religious belief and practice should not be dictated by a government had been promoted in Britain by several notable Christian leaders. Thomas Helwys in 1612 wrote, "None should be punished either with death or bonds, for transgressing against the spiritual ordinances of the New Testament, such offices ought to be punished only with the spiritual sword and censures" (meaning the word of God and the church). Also he said, "The king 'hath no power over ye immortal soules of his subjects. . . . If the King have authority to make spiritual Lords and lawes then he is an an immortall God and not a mortall man.'"[8] At about the same time, someone in the Massachusetts Bay Colony "drew up a confession of faith in which he wrote, 'The magistrate is not by virtue of the office to meddle with religion or matters of conscience, to force and compel men to this or that form of religion or doctrine, but to leave the Christian religion free to every man's conscience.'"[9]

When some the new immigrant groups in New England formed congregations that explicitly renounced the right of the state to intrude into Christian teachings and rituals they were marginalized by the community and even persecuted. Most people in the colony believed these groups were undermining the authority

5. Matt 22:37–39.
6. Gal 5:13.
7. Gal 5:22–23.
8. "Mistery of Iniquity," quoted in Verduin, *Anatomy of a Hybrid*, 221–22.
9. Verduin, *Anatomy of a Hybrid*, 221.

of their government. In 1651, Obadiah Holmes would be arrested and flogged in Boston for contesting the state rule requiring children that had been born in the colony be baptized.[10] John Cotton had only shortly before this declared in a sermon, "Denying infant baptism would overthrow all; it is a capital offense, and they are soul-mertherers."[11]

ROGER WILLIAMS OBJECTS TO COLONY RELIGION

The disputations over the colony's right to enforce Christian rules was alive when, in 1631, a cleric named Roger Williams arrived in Massachusetts Bay Colony. Williams had been ordained in the Church of England but while at Cambridge had become a Puritan, which required him to relinquish any hope of a future with that church. Moreover, he dissented from the common view in England that the state had the right to interfere in the religious affairs of its citizens. Once he had come to America these same views brought him into conflict with colony policy. When he was invited to serve in the pulpit of the church of Boston while the pastor was away, he refused because it was "unseparated." That is, the church recognized the authority of the colony over its affairs. This was a practice that Williams challenged. He argued that colony officials had no right to act against behavior that infringed against the laws of the church. Religious regulations were to be enforced only within the church itself, not by the local government. Offending one of the Ten Commandments such as adultery, violating the Sabbath, worshipping false gods, and so on, were matters for the church to enforce. Citizens who were not part of the church should be free of government policies on church matters. People needed to follow their own convictions on such issues. God, he said, "requireth not an uniformity of religion to be enacted and enforced in any civil state." In fact, he said, such "enforced uniformity, sooner or later, is the greatest occasion of civil war, ravishing

---

10. Verduin, *Anatomy of a Hybrid*, 241. See also "Obadiah Holmes."
11. Verduin, *Anatomy of a Hybrid*, 242.

consciences, persecution of Christ Jesus in His servants, and of the hypocrisy and destruction of millions of souls."[12] Notice his language: state involvement in church affairs constituted a ravishing of conscience, or, as he said in another place, "soul rape."

He did not oppose civil government as such. He acknowledged that "the Ordinances of the Magistracie to be properly and adequately fitted by God, to preserve the civill State in civill peace and order"; but God "hath also appointed a spiritual Government and Governours in matters pertaining to his worship and the consciences of men, both [being] . . . essentially distinct."[13] Obligations to government differed from obligations to one's conscience.

WILLIAMS ESTABLISHES A NEW COLONY

The debates became ever more intense and in 1635, four years after his arrival in Boston, the colony officials forced Williams with his wife and child to leave the colony. According to the clergymen involved in the trial Williams was "guilty and deserving of banishment from the colony for maintaining 'that the civil magistrate might not intermeddle even to stop a church from heresy and apostasy.'"[14] It was a severe winter.

A group of Native Americans living nearby saved Williams and his family. He was able eventually to buy land from a local tribe and he named it Providence Plantations. Eventually, he was able to go back to England to seek his own royal charter. Britain was in turmoil at the time but eventually, in July, 1663, he obtained a royal charter for a colony. The wording of the charter was significant. It "guaranteed an unprecedented level of religious liberty." Rhode Island, it said, would be a refuge for all who were "persecuted for their consciences' sake." The charter gave "a full liberty in religious concernments. . . . No person within the said colony, at any time hereafter, shall be anyway molested, punished,

---

12. Williams, "Bloody Tenant," para. 1.
13. Verduin, *Anatomy of a Hybrid*, 234.
14. Verduin, *Anatomy of a Hybrid*, 230.

disquieted, or called in question, for any differences in opinion in matters of religion."[15] "Liberty of conscience" was guaranteed.

THE RHODE ISLAND SOLUTION

One hundred twenty years later this charter would essentially become the source of the First Amendment of the United States Constitution. Even then the decision did not come easily. The delegates from the states debated what the national religion would be but came to loggerheads.[16] At that point the founding covenant of Rhode Island became helpful. Eventually, after more to-and-fro, they adopted the founding concept of Rhode Island, guaranteeing liberty of conscience to the citizens of the United States of America. The Dutch-American historian of Christianity Leonard Verduin stated that the First Amendment "marked a new departure in the structuring of human society." For some of the delegates this was a leap into an uncharted social world.[17]

SOURCES OF THE RIGHTS OF CONSCIENCE

Williams and the other dissenters who spoke out in the seventeenth century got their perspective from the New Testament. He was of course a preacher who helped form the Baptist Church in America. He got his perspective from Jesus, who appealed essentially to the private sensibilities of individuals, "their hearts." He called for his followers to obey his teachings sincerely. Obedience had to be authentic, of their own will. In such a case, some Christians argued, true faith, the thoughts and beliefs of the person, are unenforceable by law.

In any case, religious belief and practice seem not to have suffered under such a rule. Christianity has flourished under the

---

15. "Royal Charter (1644–1663)."
16. Verduin, *Anatomy of a Hybrid*, 246.
17. For more on the religious dimensions of the American Revolution see, inter alia, "Religion and the Founding."

government of the United States, where those who do not believe are legally accorded the free and full right to refuse.

We must not forfeit such a right so strenuously gained.

Bibliography

Accad, Martin, and Jonathan Andrews. *The Religious Other: A Biblical Understanding of Islam, the Qur'an and Muhammad.* Cumbria, UK: Langham Global Library, 2020.

Albright, W. F., and C. S. Mann. *Matthew.* Anchor Bible 26. Garden City, NY: Doubleday, 1971.

"Apostle Onesimus of the Seventy." Orthodox Church in America, February 15, 2025. https://www.oca.org/saints/lives/2018/02/15/100526-apostle-onesimus-of-the-seventy.

Block, Adam. "HorseHead Nebula from the Mount Lemmon SkyCenter Schulman Telescope." Wikimedia Commons, November 3, 2009. https://commons.wikimedia.org/wiki/File:IC_434_HorseHead_Nebula_from_the_Mount_Lemmon_SkyCenter_Schulman_Telescope_courtesy_Adam_Block.jpg.

Canfield, Robert L. "My God! You Are a Mussulman Man Like Me!" *On Knowing Humanity* 9 (2025). https://doi.org/10.62141/okh.v9i1.224.

"A Christian Nation? Understanding the Threat of Christian Nationalism to American Democracy and Culture." PRRI, February 8, 2023. https://www.prri.org/research/a-christian-nation-understanding-the-threat-of-christian-nationalism-to-american-democracy-and-culture.

"Countries That Still Have Slavery 2025." World Population Review. https://worldpopulationreview.com/country-rankings/countries-that-still-have-slavery.

Douglas, J. D., ed. *New Bible Dictionary.* Downers Grove, IL: Intervarsity, 1962.

Durkheim, Emile. "What Is a Social Fact?" In *Anthropological Theory: An Introductory History,* by R. Jon McGee and Richard L. Warms, 85–91. 3rd ed. Boston: McGraw Hill, 2003.

Gedeon, Joseph. "Trump's Taskforce Order Is Latest in Efforts to Boost Christian Nationalism." *Guardian,* February 7, 2025. https://www.theguardian.com/us-news/2025/feb/07/trumps-executive-order-anti-christian-bias.

Giddens, Anthony. *The Politics of Climate Change.* Cambridge, UK: Polity, 2009.

BIBLIOGRAPHY

Goldberg, Jeffrey. "Inside Jihad U: The Education of a Holy Warrior." *New York Times Magazine*, June 25, 2000. https://archive.nytimes.com/www.nytimes.com/library/magazine/home/20000625mag-taliban.html.

Ignatius. *The Epistles of Ignatius*. Aeterna, 2016. Kindle.

Jackson, Michael. *The Palm at the End of the Mind: Relatedness, Religiosity, and the Real*. Durham: Duke University Press, 2009.

James, Wendy. *The Listening Ebony: Moral Knowledge, Religion, and Power Among the Uduk of Sudan*. Oxford: Oxford University Press, 1988.

Kant, Immanuel. *The Critique of Practical Reason*. Translated by Thomas Kingsmill Abbott. Digireads, 2011. Kindle.

Kitcher, Philip. "The Climate Change Debates." *Science* 328 (2010) 1230–34.

Ladner, Keri. "The Quiet Rise of Christian Dominionism." *Christian Century* 139 (2022). https://www.christiancentury.org/article/features/quiet-rise-christian-dominionism.

Lee, Andy. "What Should We Know About the Number 12 in the Bible?" Bible Study Tools, December 21, 2023. https://www.biblestudytools.com/bible-study/topical-studies/what-should-we-know-number-12-in-the-bible.html.

Miller, Paul D. "What Is Christian Nationalism?" *Christianity Today*, February 2, 2021. https://www.christianitytoday.com/2021/02/what-is-christian-nationalism.

Mineo, Liz. "What Scares You Most About Climate Change?" Harvard Gazette, April 22, 2020. https://news.harvard.edu/gazette/story/2020/04/harvard-experts-discuss-climate-change-fears.

Munck, Johannes, trans. *The Acts of the Apostles*. Anchor Bible 31. Garden City, NY: Doubleday, 1967.

NASA/GISS. "Global Land-Ocean Temperature Index." NASA. https://climate.nasa.gov/vital-signs/global-temperature/?intent=121.

Nelson, Ryan. "How Did the Apostles Die? What We Actually Know." Overview Bible, December 17, 2019. https://overviewbible.com/how-did-the-apostles-die/.

"Obadiah Holmes." Wikipedia, last updated November 10, 2024. https://en.wikipedia.org/wiki/Obadiah_Holmes.

"Onesimus." Wikipedia, last updated July 22, 2025. https://en.wikipedia.org/wiki/Onesimus.

Oreskes, Naomi, and Erik M. Conway. *Merchants of Doubt*. London: Bloomsbury, 2010.

Piper, John. "We Are Accountable for What We Know." Desiring God, December 4, 2017. https://www.desiringgod.org/interviews/we-are-accountable-for-what-we-know.

Pocock, David. "The Ethnography of Morals." *International Journal of Moral and Social Studies* 1 (1986) 1–20.

"Religion and the Founding of the American Republic." Library of Congress. https://www.loc.gov/exhibits/religion/rel03.html.

BIBLIOGRAPHY

"Royal Charter (1644–1663)." National Park Service, last updated December 14, 2021. https://www.nps.gov/rowi/learn/historyculture/charter.htm.

Séchelles, Marie-Jean Hérault de. *Journey to Montbard*. Paris: Librairie des bibliophiles, 1890. Project Gutenberg, 2024. https://www.gutenberg.org/cache/epub/72990/pg72990-images.html.

Silver, Laura, et al. *Comparing Levels of Religious Nationalism Around the World*. Pew Research Center, January 2025. https://www.pewresearch.org/global/2025/01/28/comparing-levels-of-religious-nationalism-around-the-world/.

Stokes, Anton Phelps, ed. *Church and State in the United States*. 3 vols. New York: Harper, 1950.

Sumner, Mark. "Inside the Creepy Push to Make JD Vance America's 'Christian Prince.'" Daily Kos, September 20, 2024. https://www.dailykos.com/story/2024/9/20/2271733/-Inside-the-creepy-push-to-make-JD-Vance-America-s-Christian-Prince.

"Synagogue of the Libertines." Wikipedia, last updated March 5, 2025. https://en.wikipedia.org/wiki/Synagogue_of_the_Libertines.

Verduin, Leonard. *The Anatomy of a Hybrid*. Grand Rapids: Eerdmans, 1976.

The Westminster Standard. "Shorter Catechism: Text and Scripture Proofs." https://thewestminsterstandard.org/westminster-shorter-catechism/#Content.

Williams, Roger. "The Bloody Tenent, Of Persecution for Cause of Conscience." In *The Founders' Constitution*, edited by Philip B. Kurland and Ralph Lerner, Amendment I (Religion), doc. 4. http://press-pubs.uchicago.edu/founders/documents/amendI_religions4.html.

Index

1st Amendment in the United States, Christians and the, 129

Abimelek (king of Gerar), 97–98
Abraham, 26, 97
    denial of Sarah, 97
Adultery
    setting the scene for, 42–43
    unanswered questions about the story, 46–48
    the woman and Jesus, 45–46
    woman caught in, 40–43
Afghan War (1978–1992), the, 91
Albright, William F., 105
America, Taliban and, 91
Amos, 28
Ananias, 29
Antioch, 25
Archippus, 63, 66, **67**
Army draft, Canfield and the, 3
Assyrians, 5
Assyrian invaders, 8

Babylon, 4
Babylonian army, 8
Babylonians, siege of Jerusalem, 8–10
Bacon, Francis, 114
Bamyan Valley, 88–90
Baptism
    infant baptism, 127
    of John, 102
Baptist Church, formation of in America, 129
Beatitudes, the, 118
Believers, early, 25
Bible, science and the, 115–16
Biblical advice
    faith, 51
    love your neighbor, 55
    loving God, 53
    on nonreligious living, 49–57
Big Bang concept, 115
Bin Laden, Osama, 91
Blind, the
    claiming the promise, 15–17
    God's promise to, 3, 5
    God's promise to the Israelites, 5
Block, Adam, Horsehead Nebula, 116
Boston, Roger Williams leaving, 128
Buffon, Georges, 26

Caesarea, 77, 79
Canaan, 100
Canaanite gods, 6
Canfield, Rita, 2–3

Index

Canfield, Robert L.
  army draft and, 3
  background of, 86–90
  conversation with a farmer, 85–88, 92–95
  relationship with his wife, 2–3
Centurion, the, Peter's encounter with, 78–79
Choices, 1–2
  God and our, 2
  God's role in our, 2–3
Christianity, in the United States, 129–30
Christians
  evidence of the Pharisees and, 32–33
  finding anchorage in God, 2
  in the United States, 129–30
Christians, early, Jesus rising from the dead and, 31–32
Christ's resurrection, witnesses to, 102–3
Chronicles, 11
  explanation of the calamity, 9
  intent of the book of, 8
Church of England, 127
Climate change, 120–22
Colony religion, objections to, 127–28
Colosse, Paul's letter to the church at, 65
Colossian church, 65
Communications, improvements in, 1
Conscience, rights of, 129–30
Conway, Erik M., 121
Cornelius, 78, 79
  Peter and, 78–83
  sharing encounter with angels, 81
Cosmic microwave background radiation, 115
Cotton, John, 125, 127
Crucifixion, the days after the, 101–2
Cult prostitutes, 6

Cyrus
  defeat of the Babylonians by, 4
  invitation to the Israelites to go home, 4

Daral Uloom madrasa, 90
Dark, the
  trusting God in, 20–23
  trusting God in the dark
David, 28
Defeated, promises to the, 10–14
Deuteronomy, 6

Disciples
  behavior after Jesus's resurrection, 34–36
  choosing of the twelve, 100–106
  importance of the, 106
  Jesus calling the, 24
  Jesus choice of, 59
  persecution of, 25
Dreadful judgments, 119

Earth, warming of the, 120–22
Egypt, Moses's return to, 27
Einstein, Albert, 115
Eternal life, how to inherit, 53
Ethnography, 96
Eunuchs, Yahweh's promise to the, 14
Exilic experience, 4–5
Exodus, 28
Ezekiel, 108, 111–12

Faith
  Godly life and, 21
  listening for indications of, 23–25
  listening to God's will, 23–25
  versus religion, 23
  the walk of, 18–19
  walking in, 26–29
False witnesses, 74
Fire, tongues of, x
First Amendment, source of the, 129

Index

Foods, God's message to Peter about unclean, 79
foreigners (khārejis), 85
Founding Fathers, 124
Friedmann, Alexander, 155

Genesis, 116
   the creation story in, 113
   textual explication of, 113–17
Gentiles, God's working with, 79
Giddens, Anthony, 122–23
Global Land-Ocean Temperature Index, 120
God
   find anchorage in, 3
   as a jealous, 22
   promises of, 29–30
   trust in, 26–28
   trusting God in the dark, 20–23
   walking with, 19–20
Godliness, patience and, 26
Golden calves, the, 5
Good neighbor, Samaritan as the, 52, 57
Gospel of John, woman caught in adultery in the, 40–41
Gospel of Luke, 21
Gospel proclamation, the, 105
Greenland icecap, 120

Hazaras (1982–1984) (war), 91
Hebrew Kingdoms, collapse of, 5–10
Helwys, Thomas, 126
Hezekiah, 4
Holmes, Obadiah, 127
Holy Spirit, 100, 102
   Pentecost and the, 103
Horsehead Nebula, by Adam Block, 116
Hoyle, Fred, 155
Hubble, Edwin, 155
Hutton, James, 114

Infant baptism, 127
Iran, 91

Isaiah, 4, 20–21, 109–10
   Chapter 40 to the end of, 12–14
   dispute about chapters 40 to the end, 4–5
   God's promise to the blind, 3
   Isaiah 49, 13
Israel, decline of, 5
Israelites
   the apostasy of the, 8
   exilic situation of, 4–5
   explanation of the calamity, 11–14
   God's promise after the defeat of the, 11–12
   God's promise to, 4
   prophets' messages to, 5
Italian Regiment, 78

Jackson, Michael, 96
Jairus, daughter of, 105
James, 37
James Webb Space Telescope, 116
Jehoiakim (King), 8
Jeremiah, 6–7, 108–9
   praying for the Israelites, 7
   prosecution of, 107–8
Jeroboam, 5
Jerusalem, 5
   final humiliation of, 5–10
   Jesus weeping over, 16
   siege of, 8–10
Jesus
   his choice of disciplines, 59
   pericopes about, 105–6
   predictions of, 122–23
   questioning the woman caught in adultery, 45–46
   rising from the dead, 31
   rumors about him, 99–106
   shifting the focus from the adulterous woman, 43–45
   weeping over Jerusalem, 16
   woman caught in adultery story and, 40–41
Jewish Christians, 76

Index

Jewish Scriptures, 59
Jews
    Christianized, 79
    Gentiles and, 79–80
    God's promise to, 10–14
Jewish Christians, 76
    Jewish Scriptures, 59
    marginal, 73
    religious zeal of, 72
    and Romans, 77–78
John/Gospel of, 25
    addressing the rumors about Jesus, 99
    Baptism of John, 102
Jonah, 28–29
Joppa, 77
    Peter's experience in, 79
Jordan River, 100
Joseph, 26–27
Josiah, 6
Judah, decline of, 5–8
Judas, 24, 102
Judgments, dreadful, 119

Kabul (1992–1996), battle for, 91
Khodāhdād, 91
    Robert L. Canfield's conversation with, 92–95
    seen in a biblical context, 97–98
King Jehoiakim, 8
Kitcher, Philip, 121–22

Laodicean Church, the problem of the, 16
Lemaître, Georges, 115
listening, life of faith and, 23–25
Luke/Gospel of, 21, 78
    story in the book of Acts, 78–79
    Sermon on the Mount in, 118
Lyell, Charles, 114

Malachi, 112
Manasseh, 5
Mann, C. S., 105
Marginal Jews, 73

Mark's Gospel, 118
Martyrdom, of Stephen, 25
Mary Magdalene, 33–34, 36
Massachusetts Bay Colony, 125, 127
    confession of faith in, 126
Mathematical Principles of Natural Philosophy (Newton), 114
Matthew/Gospel,
    thoughts about treating others, 59
    Sermon on the Mount in, 118
Matthias, 24
    choosing of, 102
Merchants of Doubt, 121
Messiah, the crucifixion of, 104
Meyer, A. J., 122
Micah, 110
Modern society, impact on technology on, 1–2
Moral personhood, 96
Mosaic tradition, 6
Moses, life of faith of, 27–28
Mujahedin organizations, funding of, 91
Mussulman/*Musulmān*, 95–96
    conversation with the author, 85–88

Nations, God and people from every, 76–77
Native Americans, rescue of Roger Williams, 128
Natural philosophy, 114
Nehemiah, 29
Neighbor, loving your, 55
New Testament, 126
    slavery in the, 58–60
Newton, Isaac, *Mathematical Principles of Natural Philosophy*, 114
Non-Jewish communities, 25
Nonreligious living, biblical advice on, 49–57
Northern Alliance, 91

Index

Old Testament, 107
Old Testament prophets, as social critics, 107
Olivet Discourse, the, 118
    Luke's version of, 118–20
Onesimus, 60–64, 67–71
    effect of Jesus's death and resurrection on, 69–71
Opportunities, broadening of, 1–2
Oreskes, Naomi, 121

Patience, 26
Paul, 21, 29, 126
    as defender of Christianity, 38–39, 59
    individuals with, **66**
    letter to the church at Colosse, 65
    and Philemon, 60–65
    slavery and, 58–60
Pentecost, Holy Spirit and, 103
Penzias, Arno, 155
Pericopes, 105–6
Persians, defeat of the Babylonians by, 4
Personhood, moral, 96
Peter, 25, 37, 76–77, 79
    being with Gentiles, 80–84
    Cornelius and, 78–79, 78–83
    his great declaration, 76–77
    raising women from the dead, 77
    talking about Pentecost and the last Passover, 103–4
Pharaoh, Joseph story and, 27
Pharisaic tradition, 18–19
Pharisaism, 23
Pharisees, evidence of the, 32–34
Philemon
    effect of Jesus's death and resurrection on, 69–71
    first letter to, 60–65
    Paul and, 60–65
    second letter to, 65–69
Philosophy, natural, 114
Pilate, 33

Pocock, David, 96
Politics, use of religious zeal and, 72–75
Primeval atom, 115
Promise
    claiming the, 15–17
    God's promise the Israelites, 11–12
Prophesies, in the Old Testament, 107–12
Prophets
    critical descriptions of man's betrayal, 108–12
    messages to the Israelites, 5, 10
    as social critics, 107
    treatment of, 5
Prostitutes, cults, 6
Provenance, 41
Providence Plantations, 128
Psalms, Messianic promises in the, 104
Public Religion Research Institute, 125

Queen of Heaven, the, 6

Religion
    versus faith, 23
    political uses of, 72–75
    state, 125–26
Religious regulations, 127
Resource poor, 1
Resurrection, the, 32 34
    witnesses to, 102–3
Rhode Island, 128
    impact on the First Amendment, 129
Rhode Island Solution, the, 129
Rights of Conscience, 129–30
Romans, and Jews, 77–78
rough times, 20

Samaria, 8

Index

Samaritan/Samaritans, 57
   conversion of, 25
   as a good neighbor, 52, 57
   Stephen as a, 73
Sarah, 97
Saul. *see also* Paul
   accessory to Stephen's death, 37
   conversion of, 25, 29
   persecution of Christians by, 37–38
Saul of Tarsus. *see* Saul
Science
   complementary to the creation story, 115–16
   explanation of, 114
Sermon on the Mount, 118
Shorter Westminster Catechism, 97
Sightlessness
   God's promises and, 22
   reasons for, 15
Simon the Zealot, 59
Slavery, New Testament writers on, 58–60
Social critics, Old Testament prophets as, 107
Solomon
   destruction of the temple, 11
   temple of, 4, 6
Son of Man, coming of, 119
Soviet invasion, 91
Spiritual walk, 19–20
State religion, struggle over in the United States, 125–26
Stavins, Robert N., 122
Stephen
   false witnesses against, 74
   Jews of the Synagogue of the Freedmen and, 73–75
   martyrdom of, 25
   as a Samaritan/Samaritans, 73
   Saul and his death, 37
   Synagogue of the Freedmen and, 73–75
Synagogue of the Freedmen, Stephen and the, 73–75
Synoptic Gospels, the Olivet Discourse, 118

Taliban, 91
Technology, modern society and, 1–2
Ten Commandments, 72
   church enforcement of, 127–28
   as emblems of public virtues, 74
   living by the standards of the, 72
   Roger Williams and the enforcement of the, 128
Tongues of fire, 103
Tophet, 6
Torah, the, 6
Transportation, improvements in, 1
Twelve
   importance of the, 106
   significance of, 100–106
Twelve men, Jesus choosing the, 100–106
Tychicus, 66, **67**

Unclean foods, God's message to Peter and, 79
Uniformitarianism, 114, 116
United Nations Climate Change Conference, Copenhagen, 123
United States
   as a Christian nation, 124–25
   Christianity in the, 129–30
   state religion in, 125–26
United States Constitution, 129
Unknown, stepping into, 20–23
Unmarried women, 14

Valley of Achor, 22
Verduin, Leonard, 129
Voltaire, 116

Walk, the
   faith and walking with God, 18–19
   spiritual walk, 19–20
   the walk of faith, 19–20

Index

Whewell, William, 114
Wilderness, the march through the, 28
Williams, Roger, 127–28
    establishment of a new colony, 128
    formation of the Baptist Church in America, 129
    leaving Boston, 128
Wilson, Robert, 155
Witnesses, false, 74

Women,
    unmarried, 14
    Yahweh's message to, 14

Yahweh, 22–23
    message to unmarried women, 14
    pollution of the sanctuary of, 5–6
    unfaithfulness to, 5
Young Life, 86

Zedekiah, 8

www.ingramcontent.com/pod-product-compliance
Lightning Source LLC
Chambersburg PA
CBHW072145160426
43197CB00012B/2252